Black Kings and Queens
Coloring Book

Adult Colouring Books

Aryla Publishing 2020

978-1-912675-75-3

www.arylapublishing.com

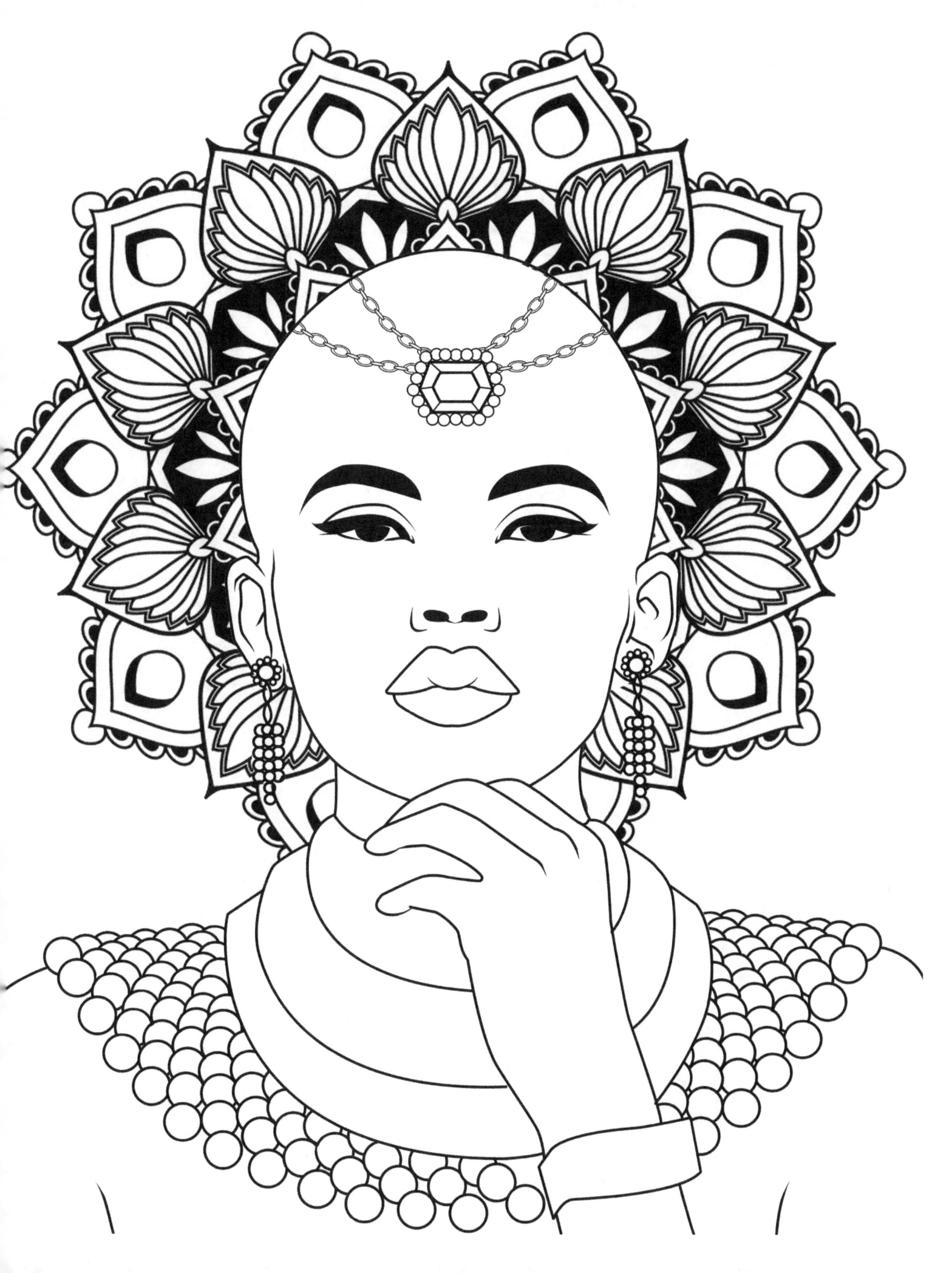

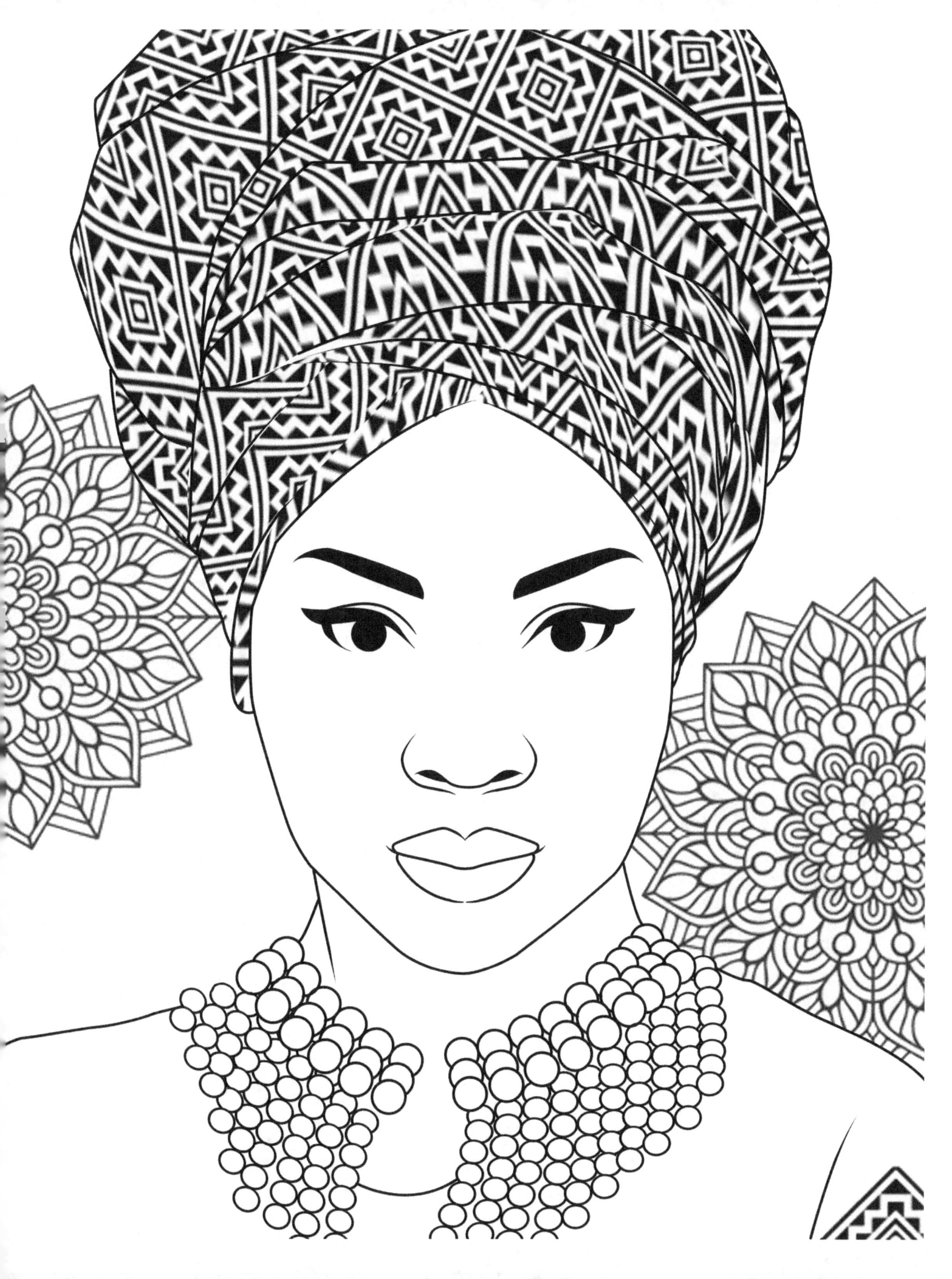

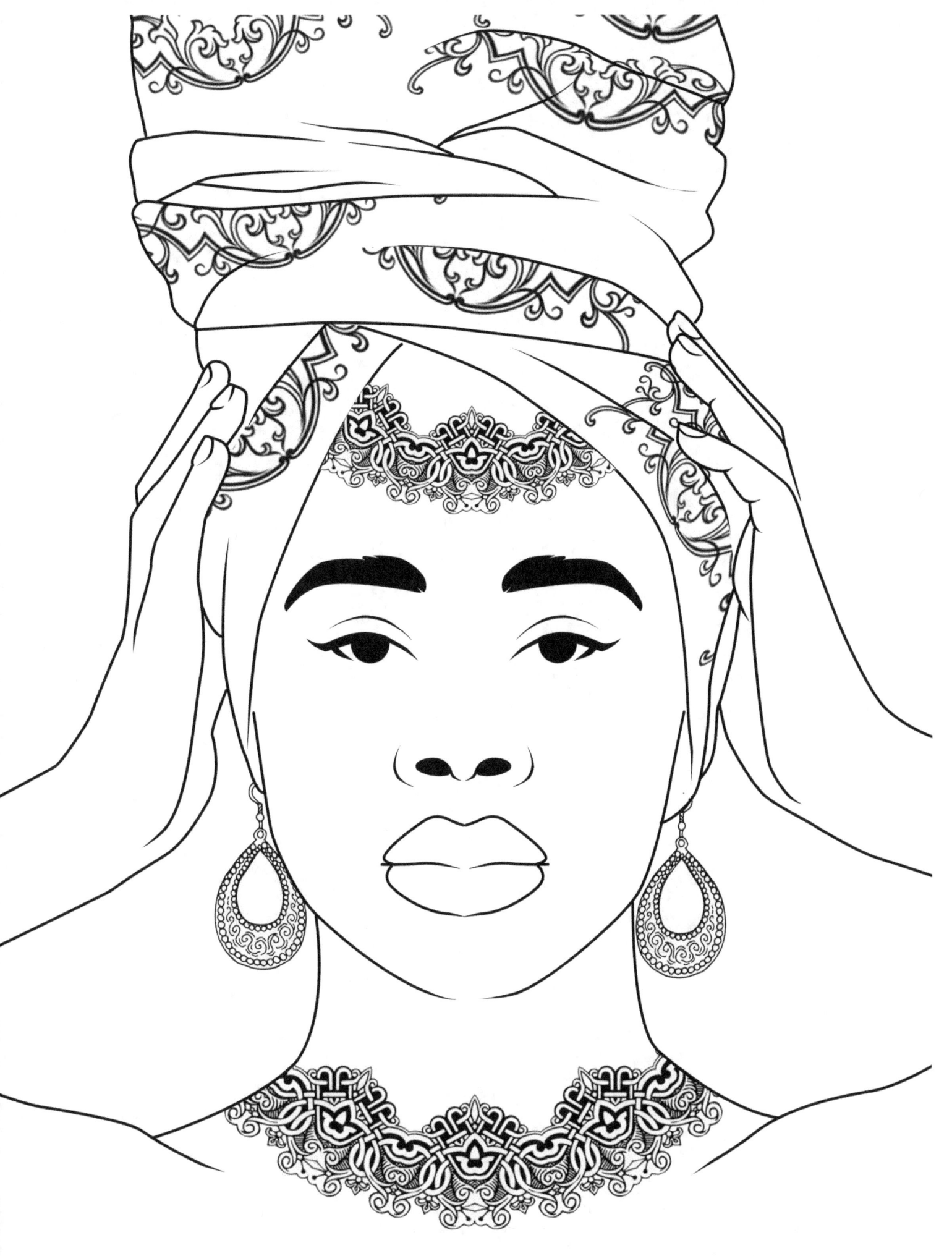

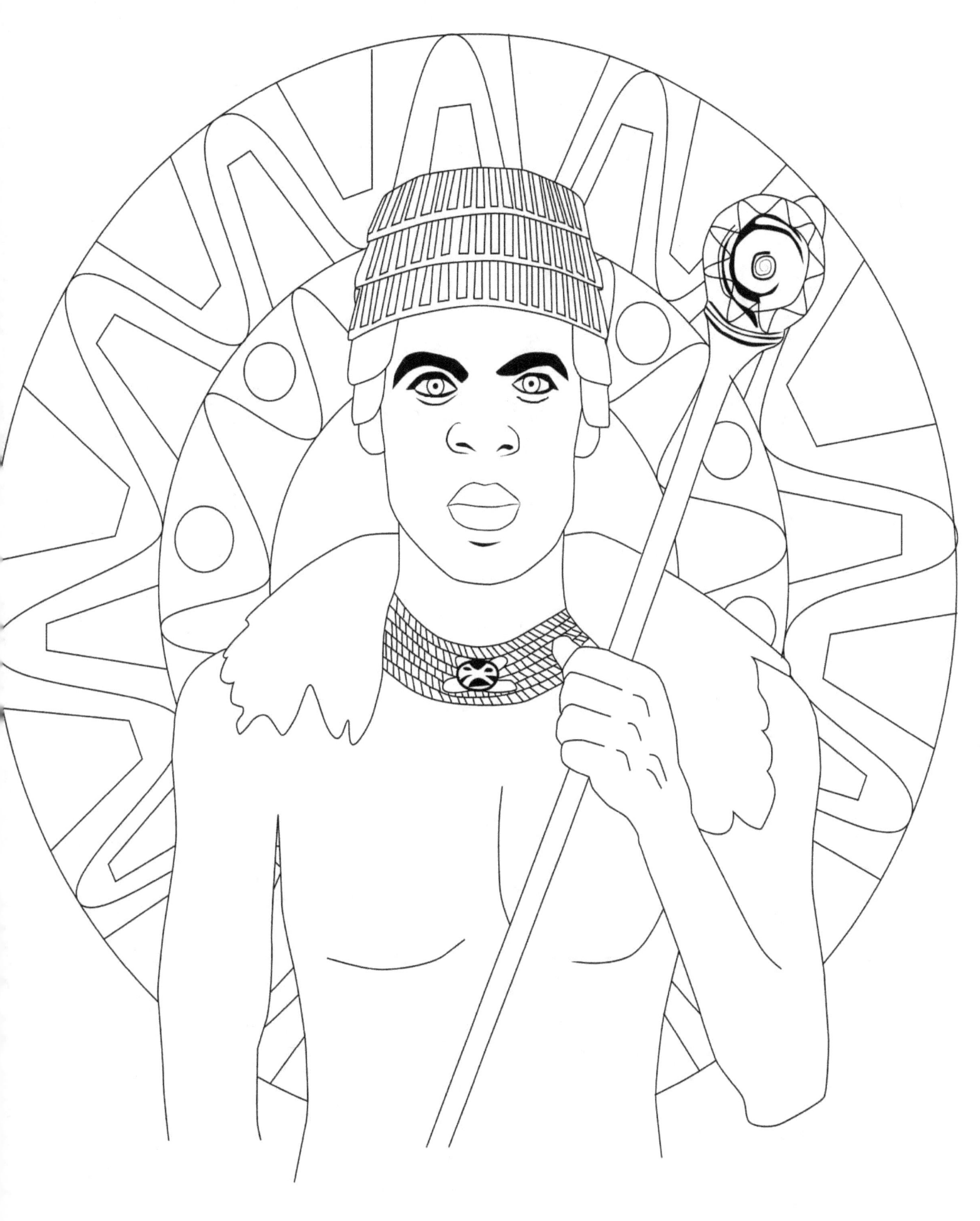

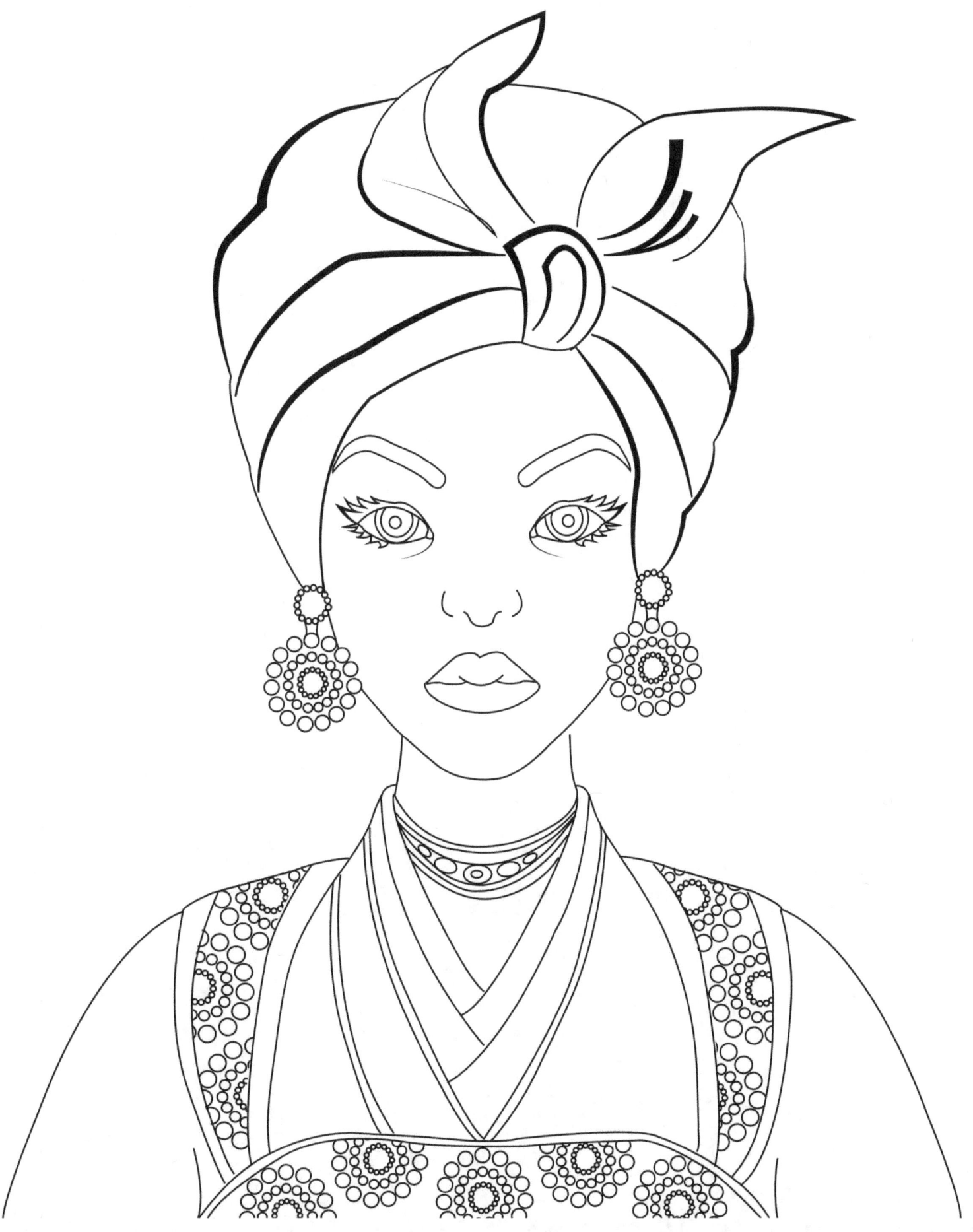

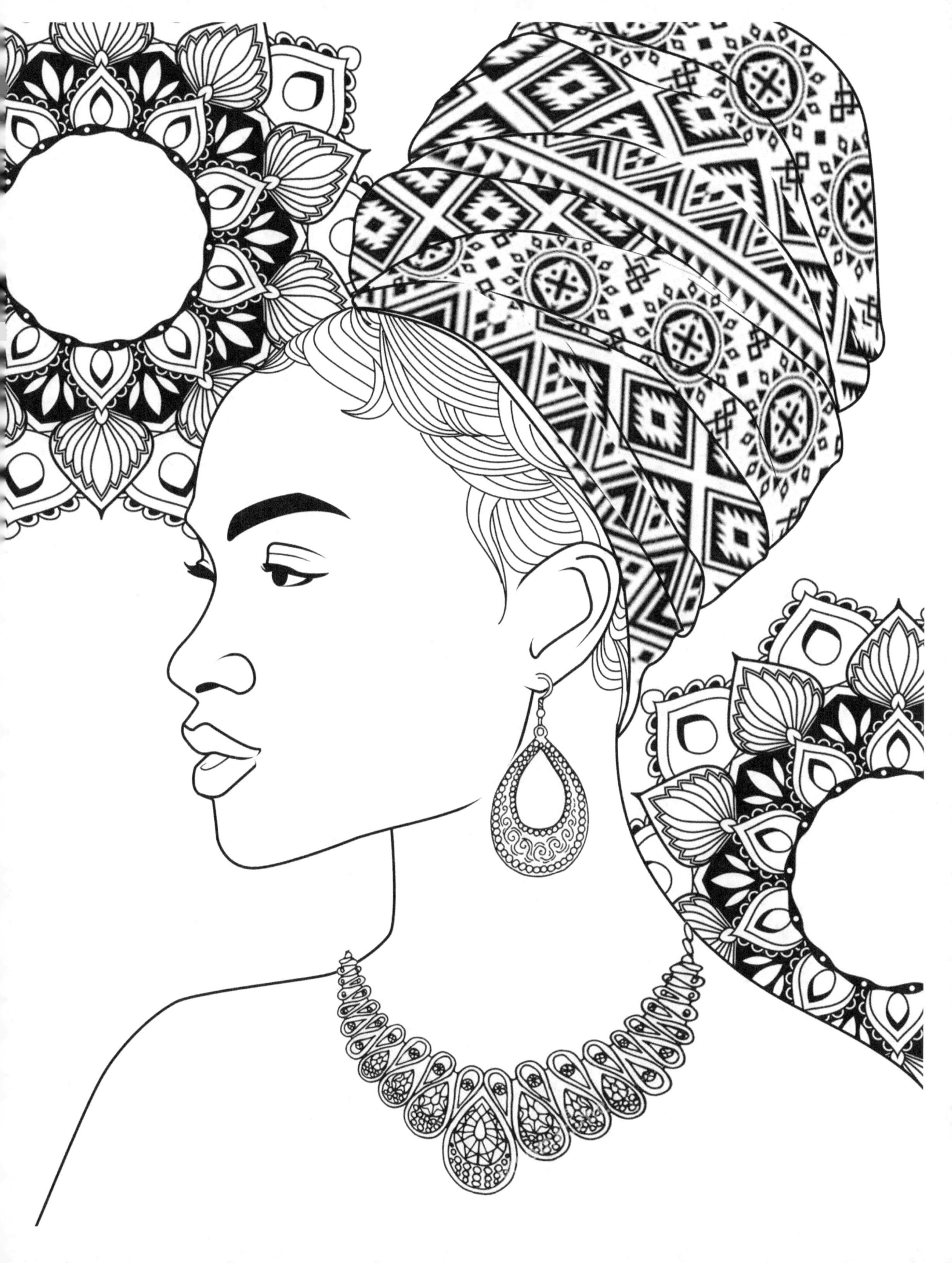

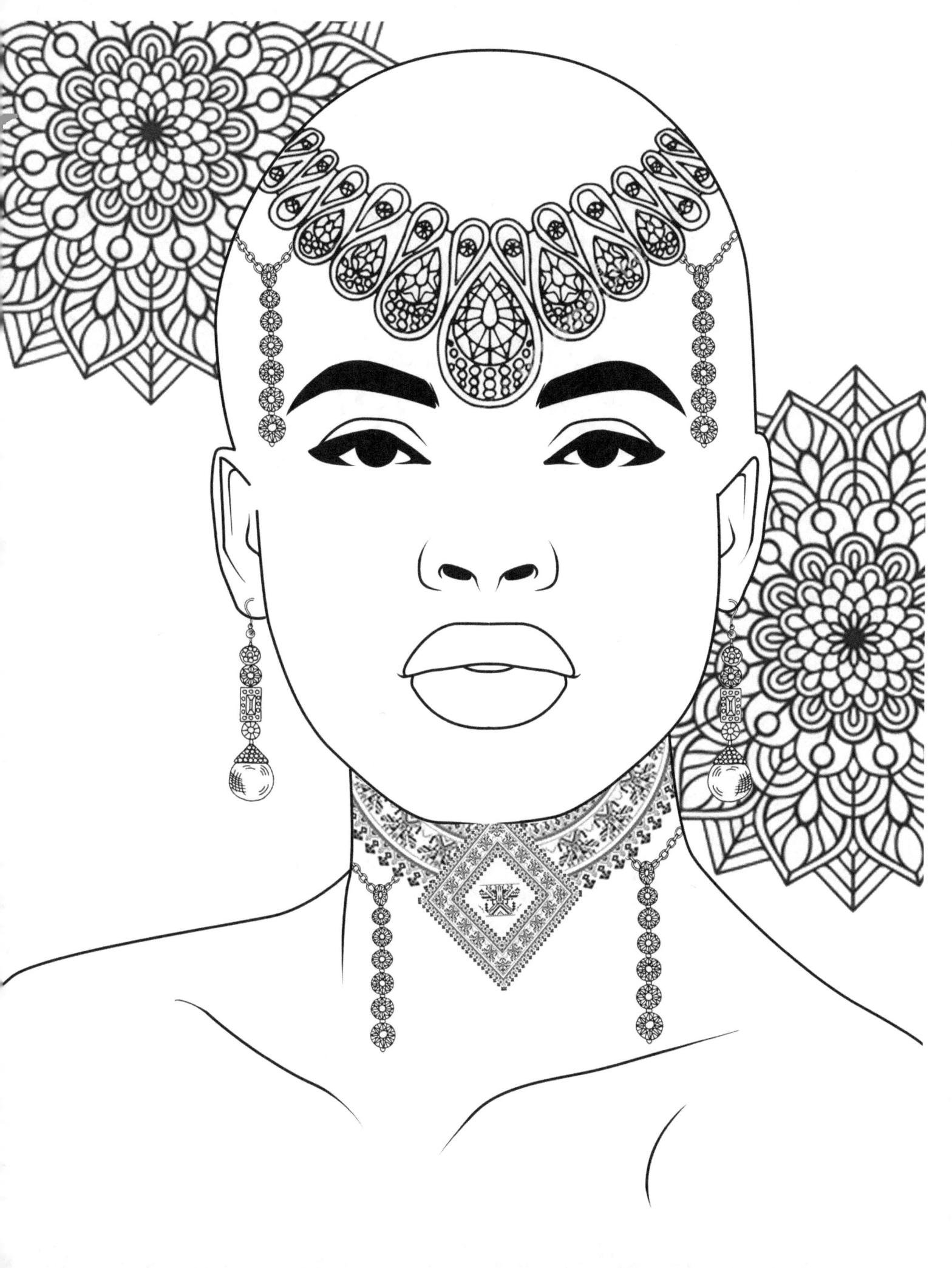

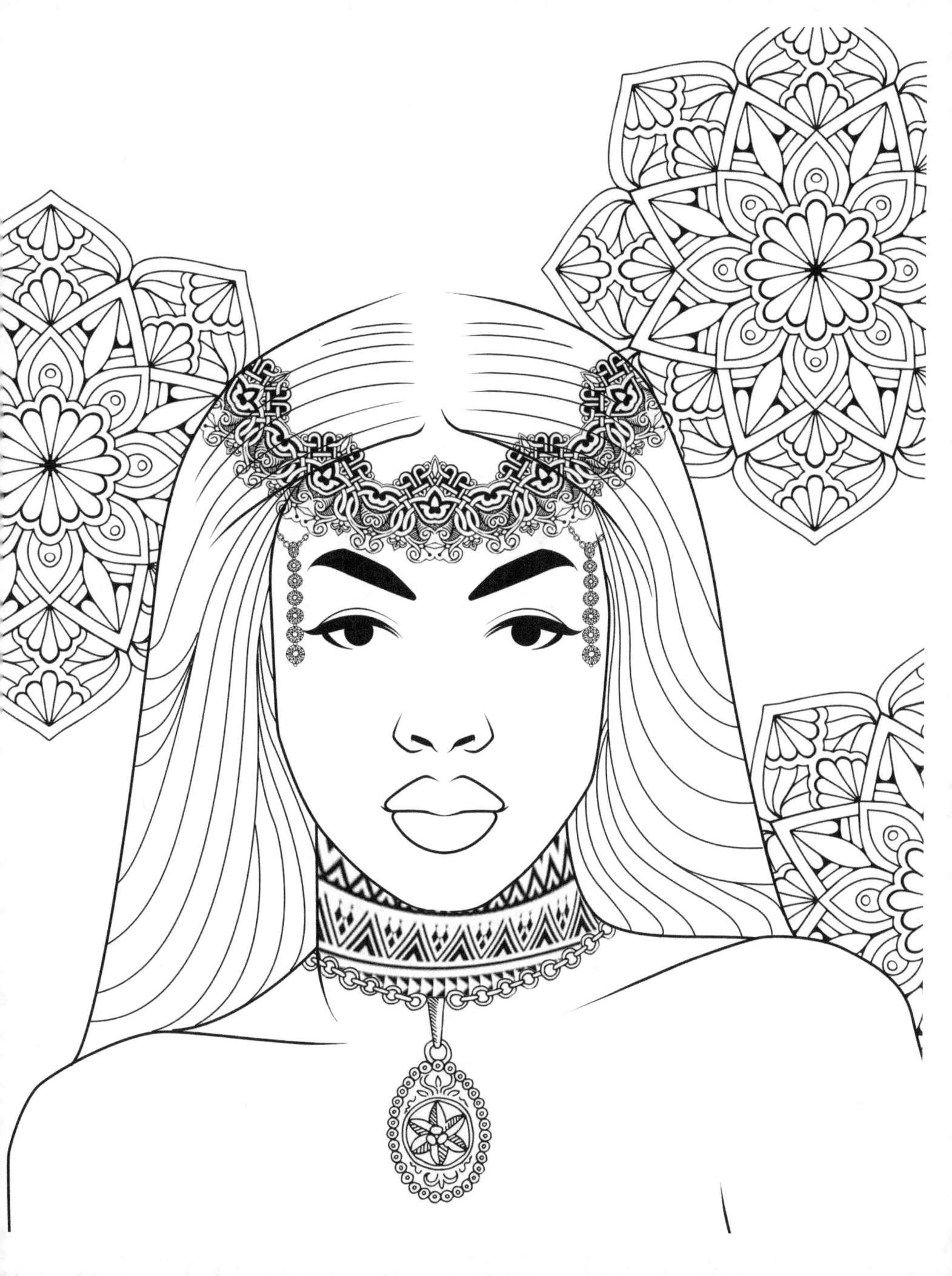

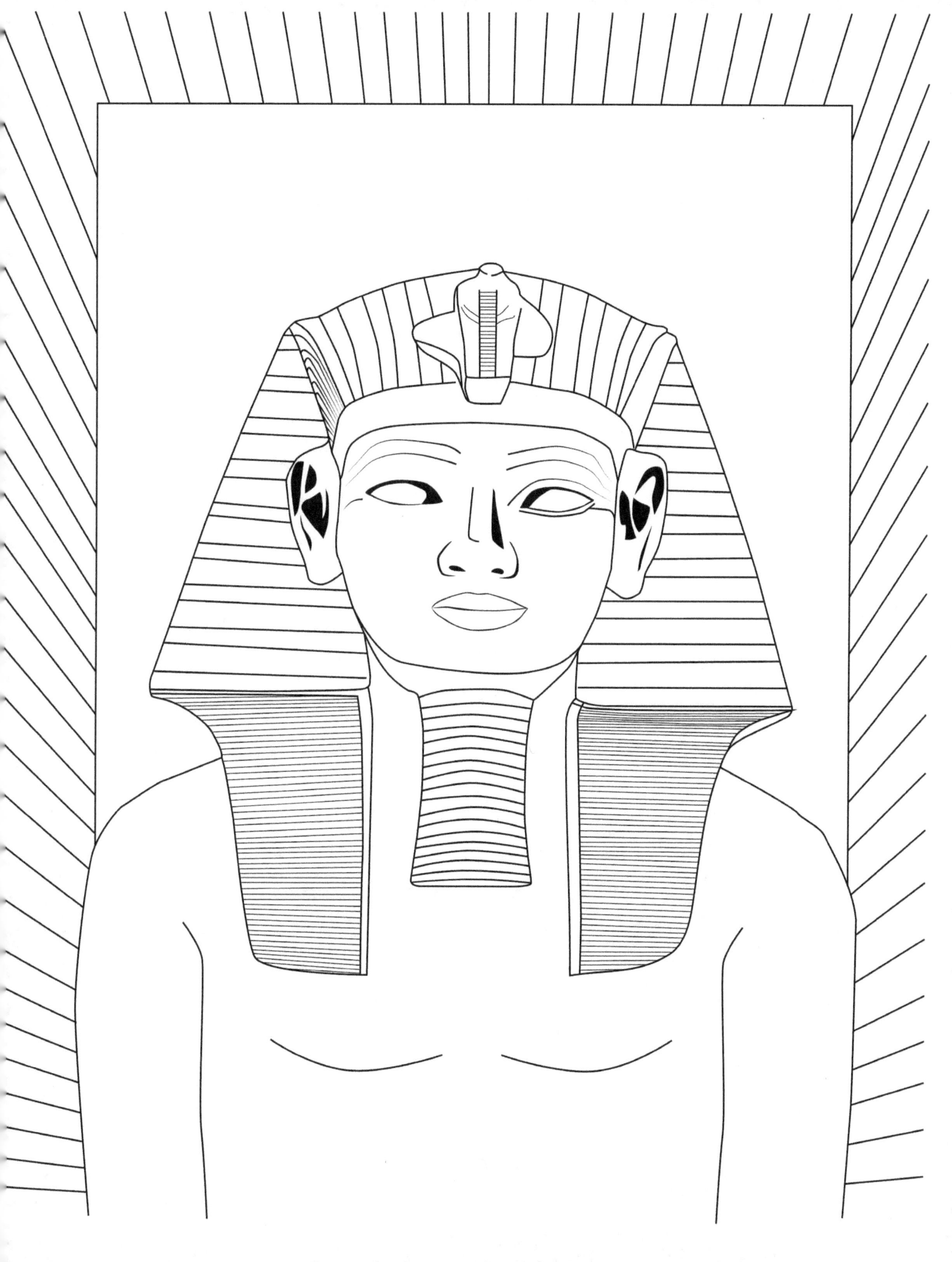

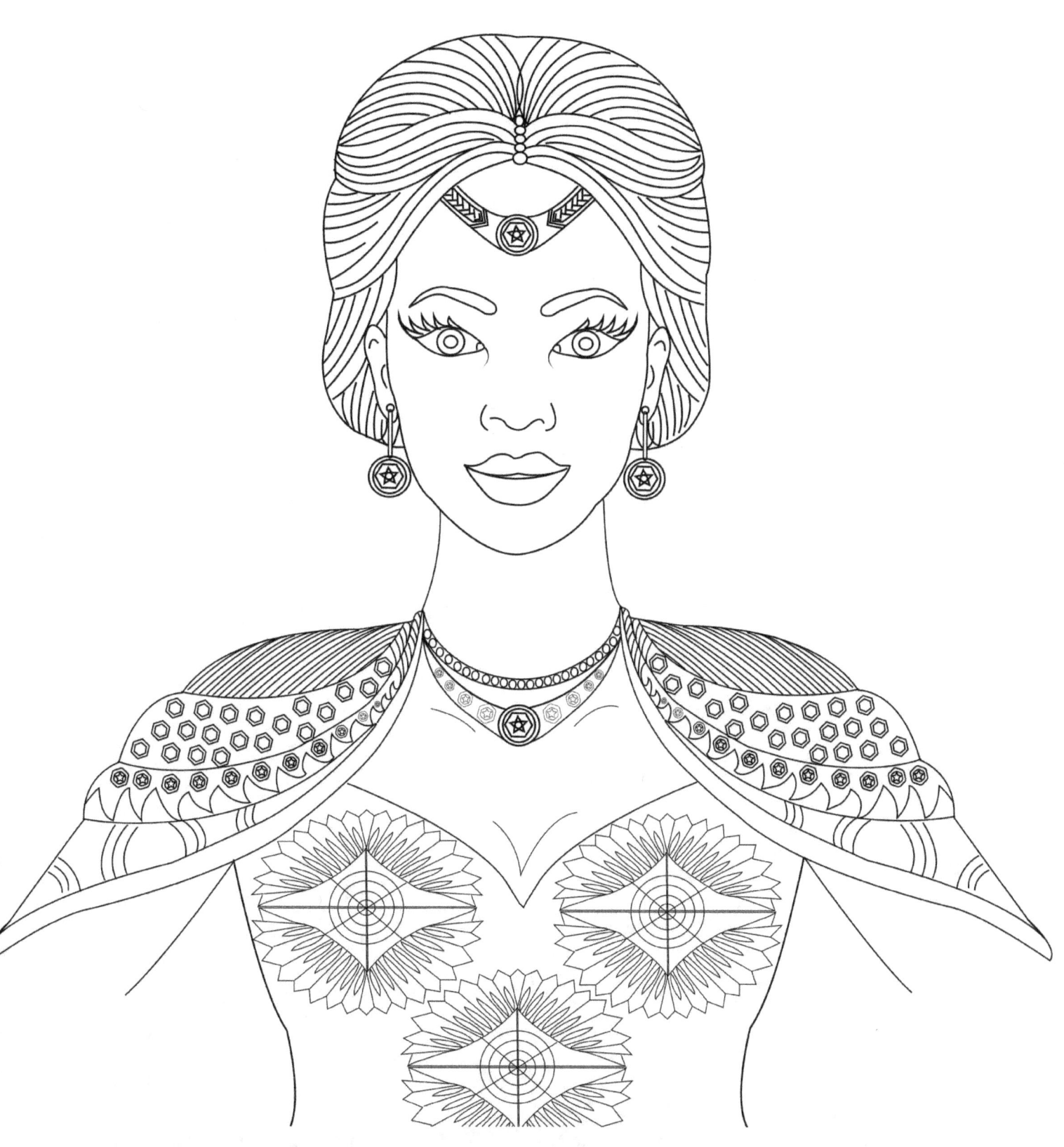

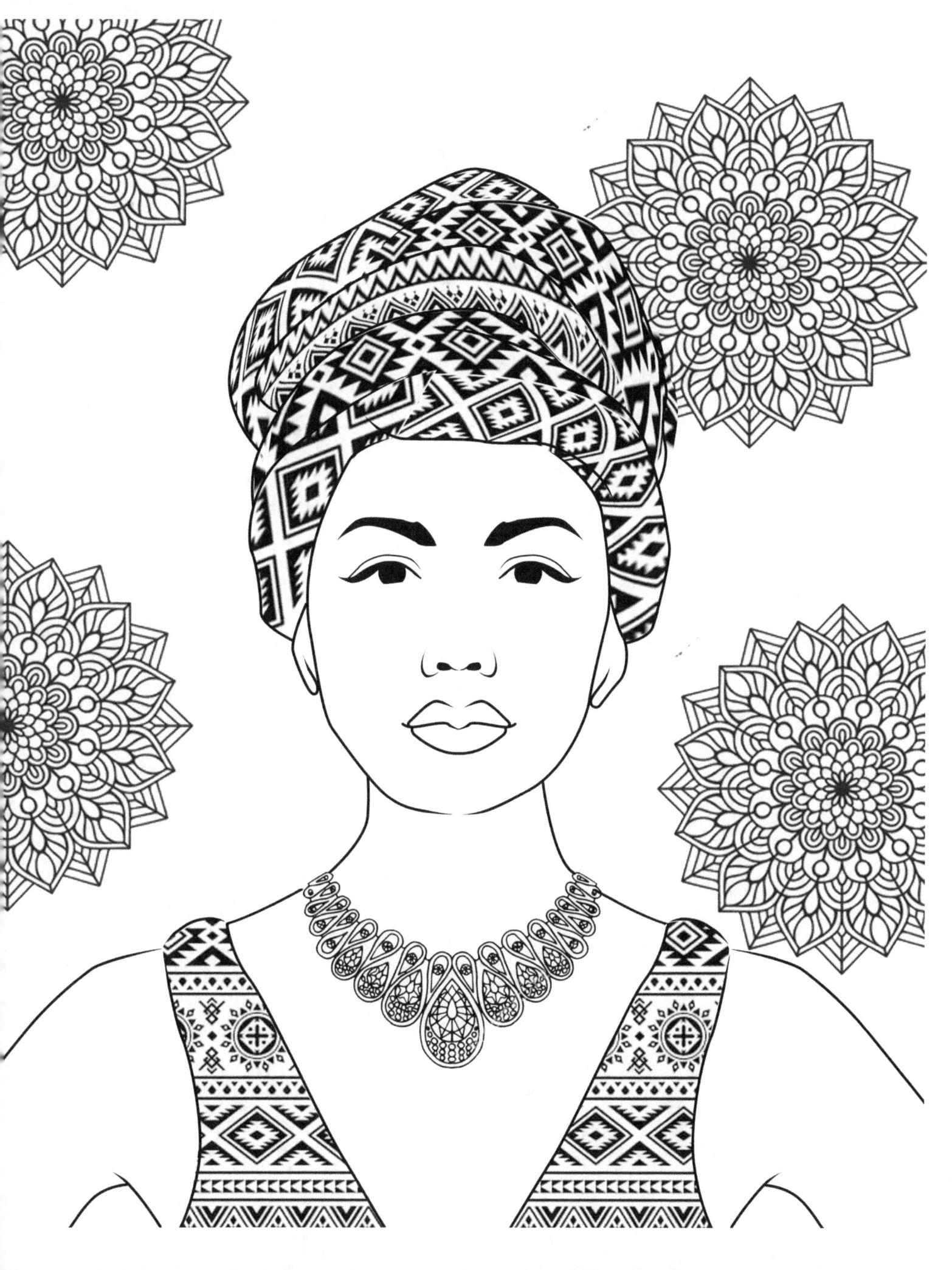

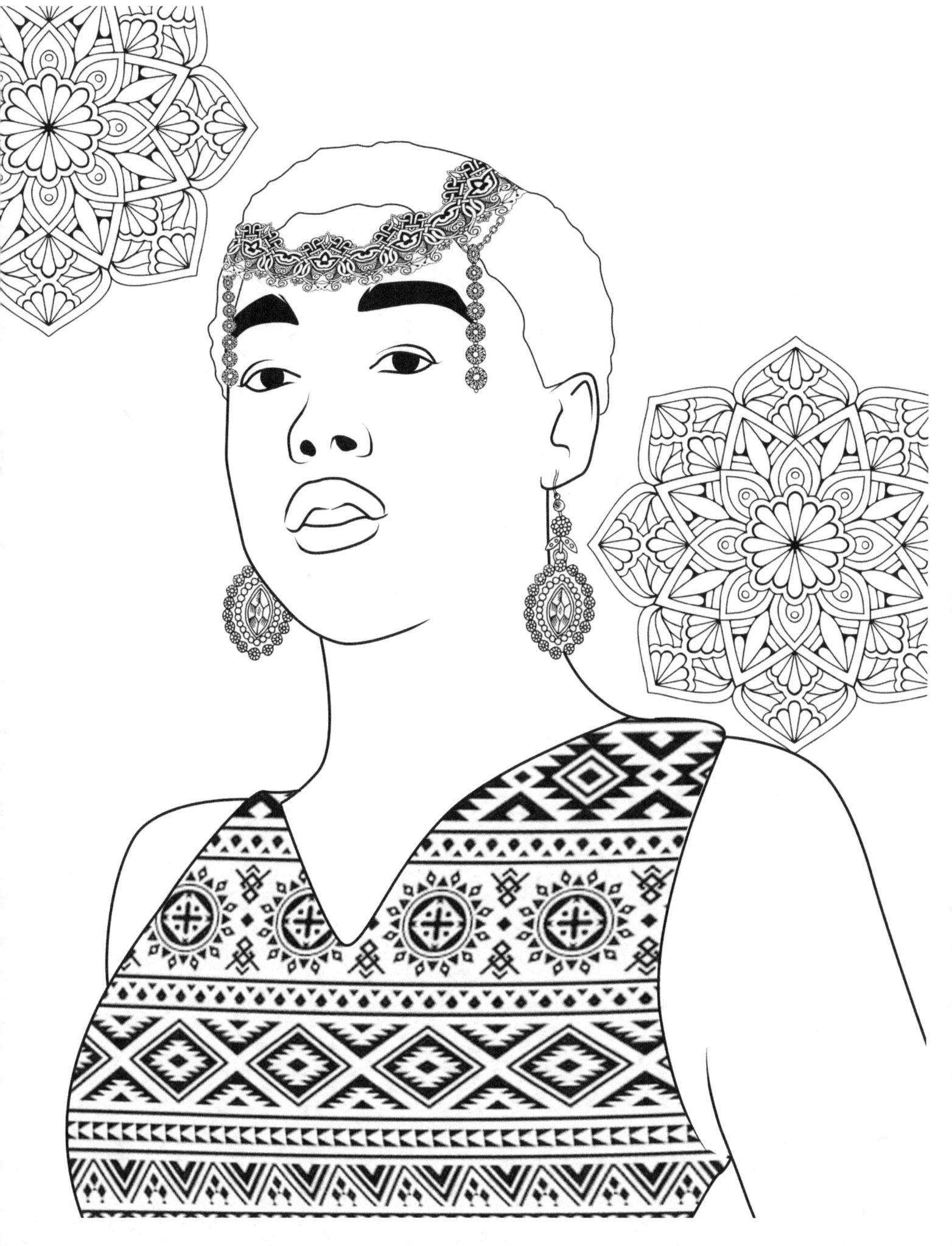

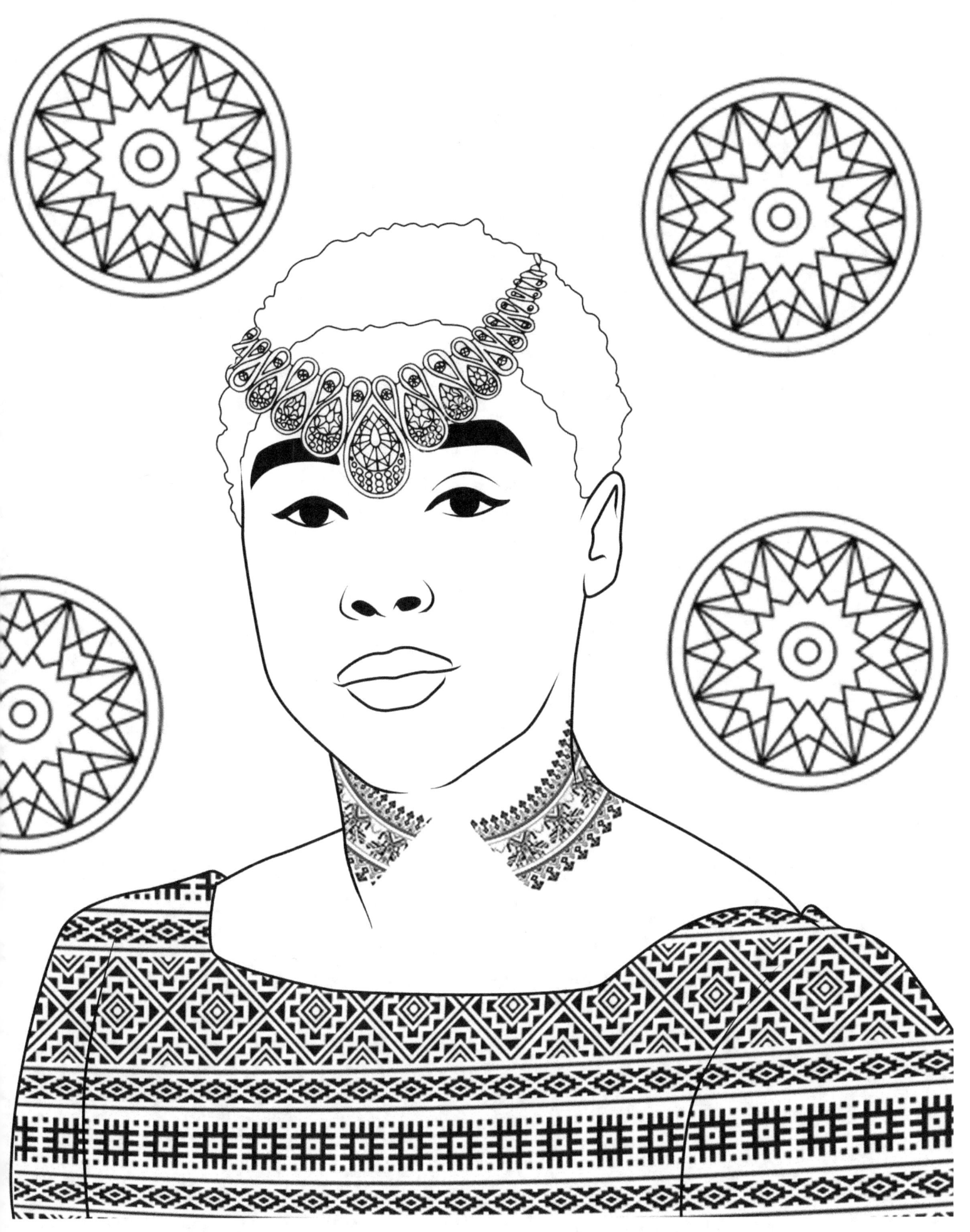

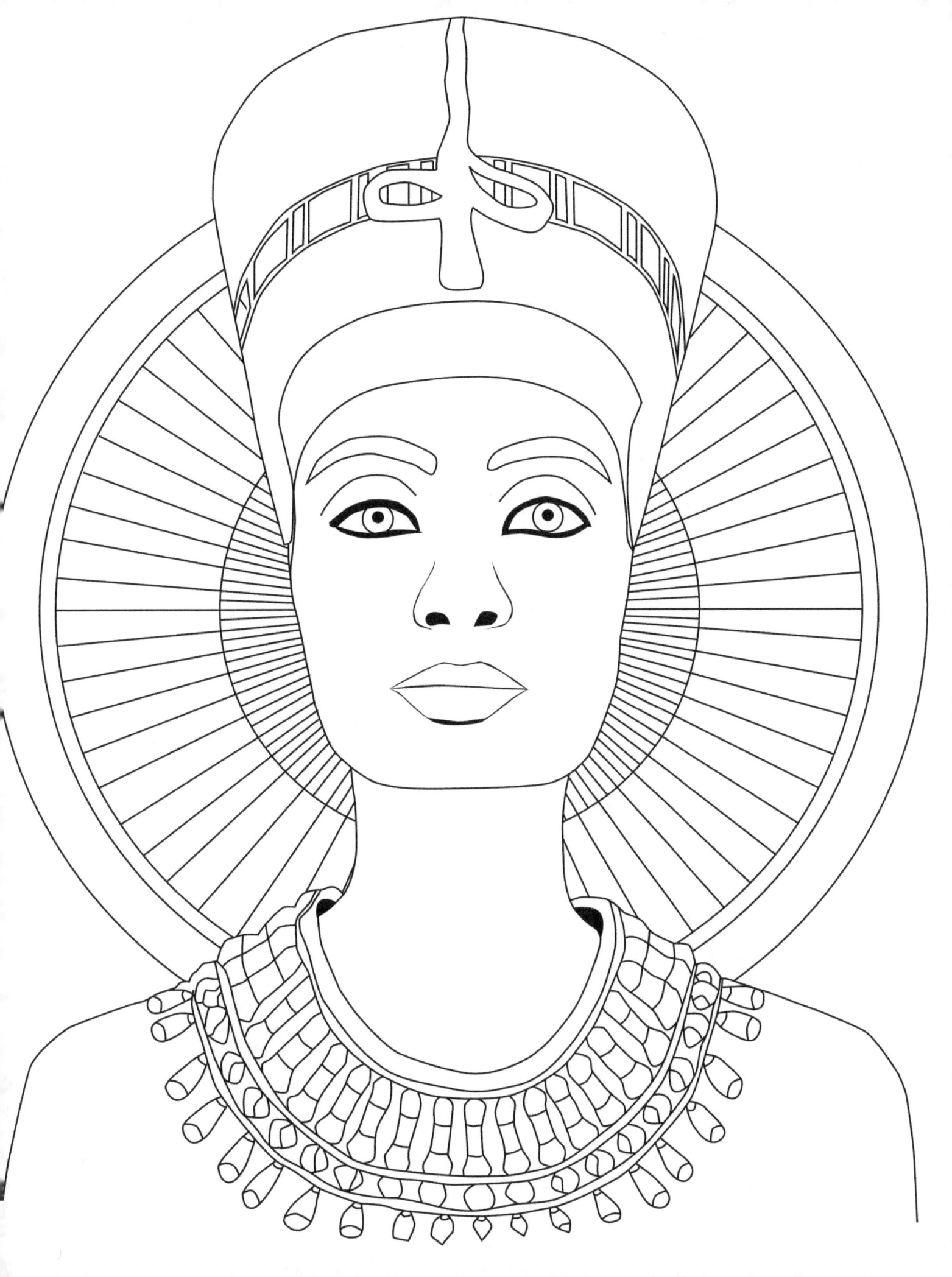

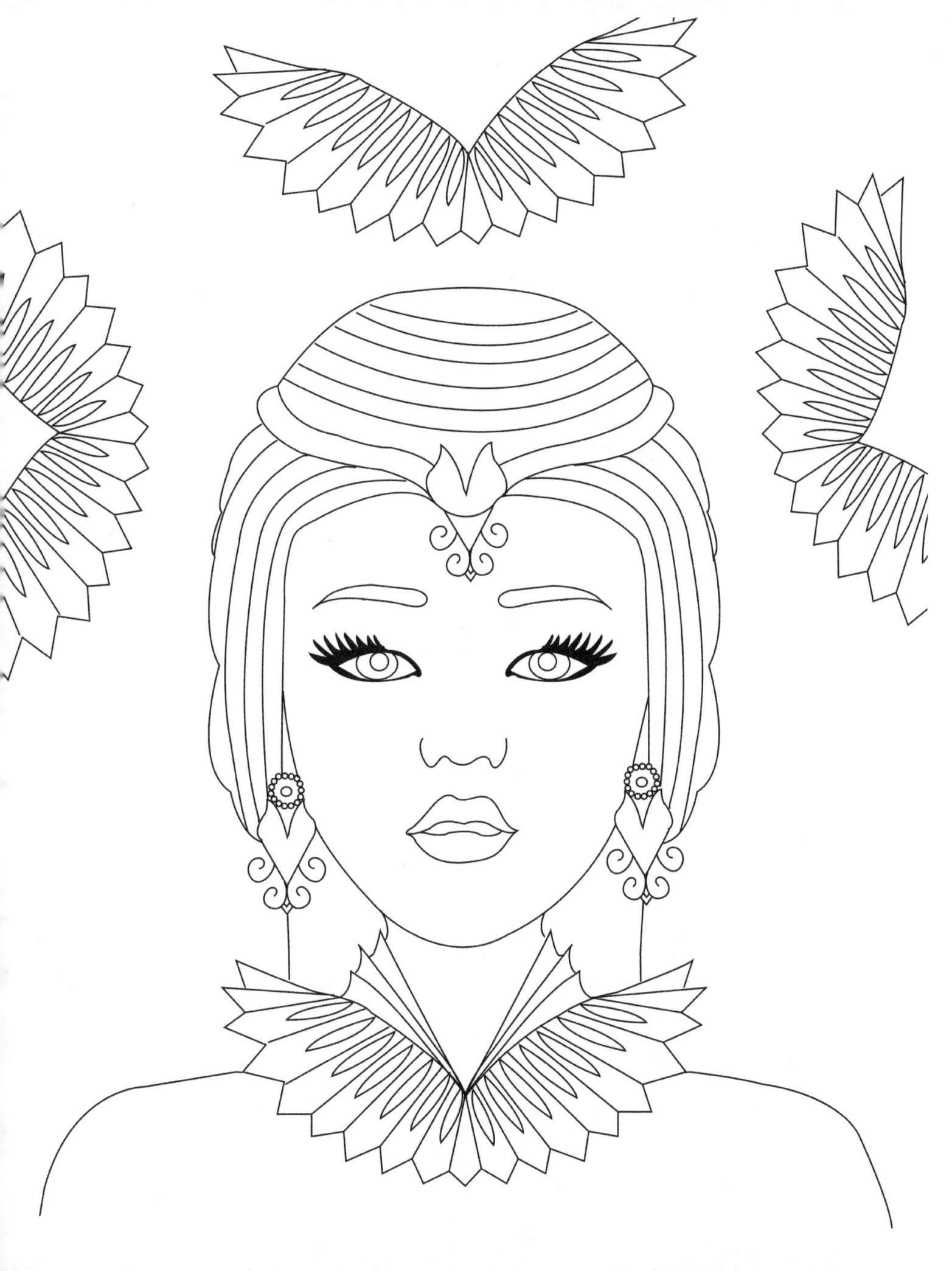

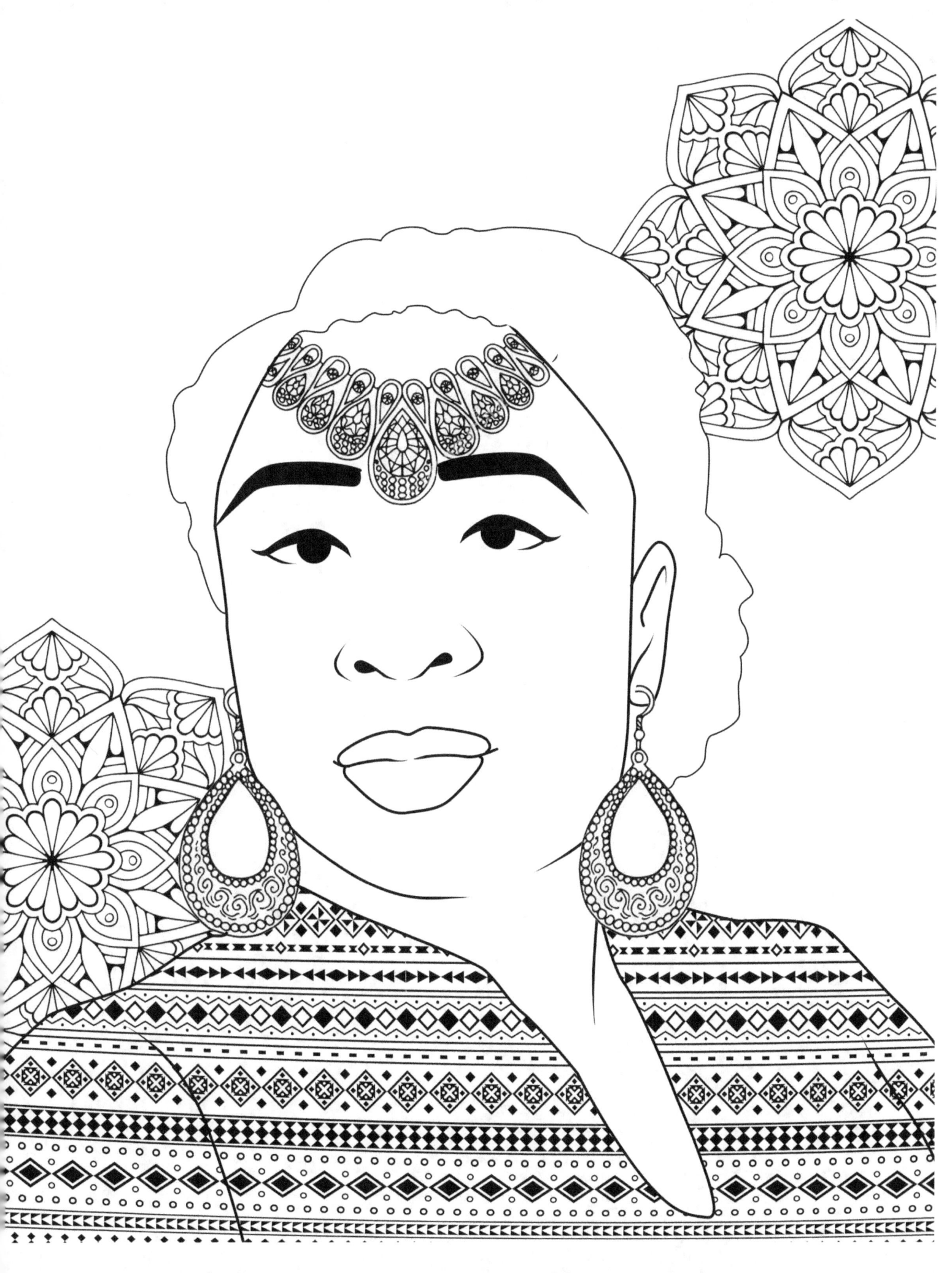

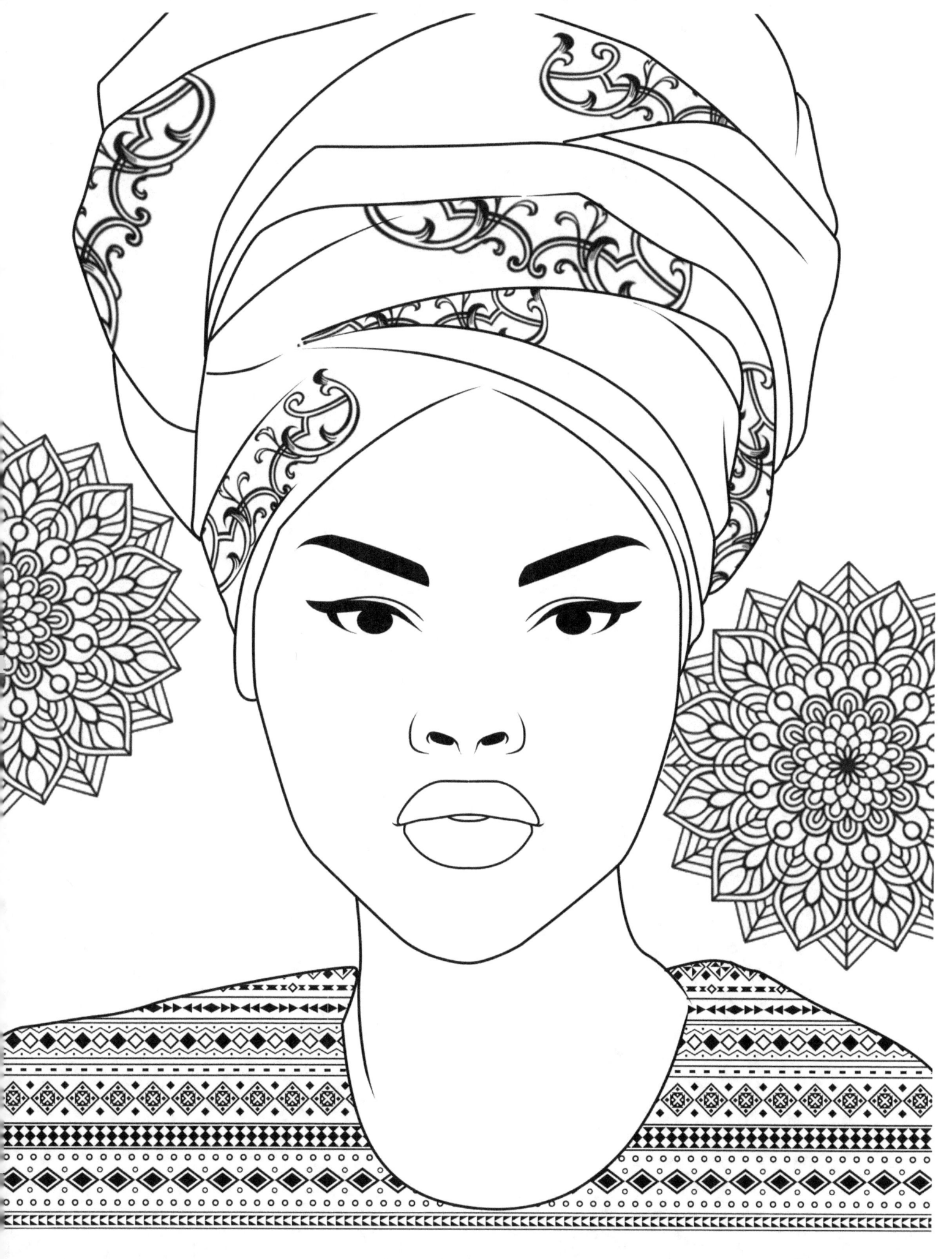

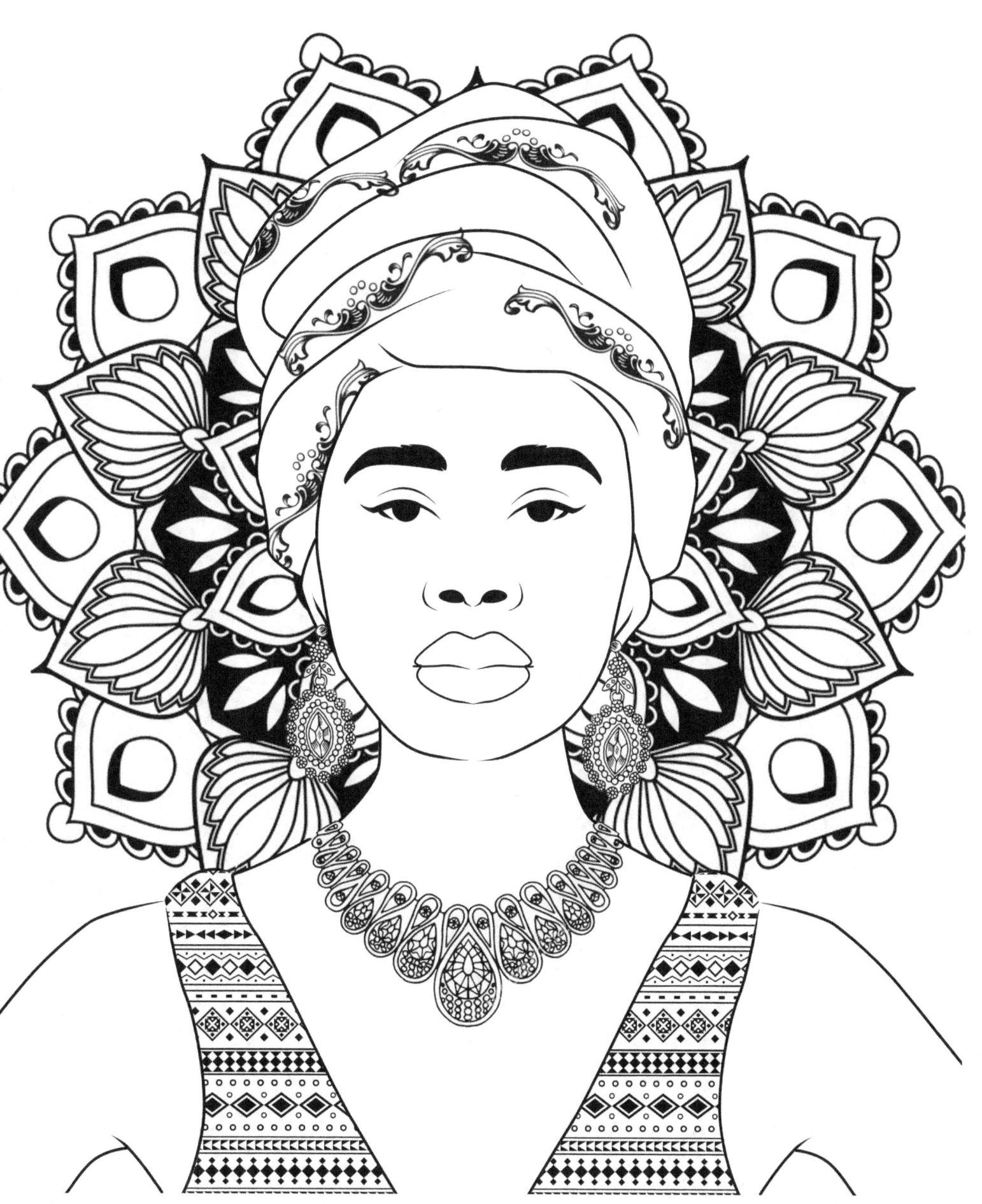

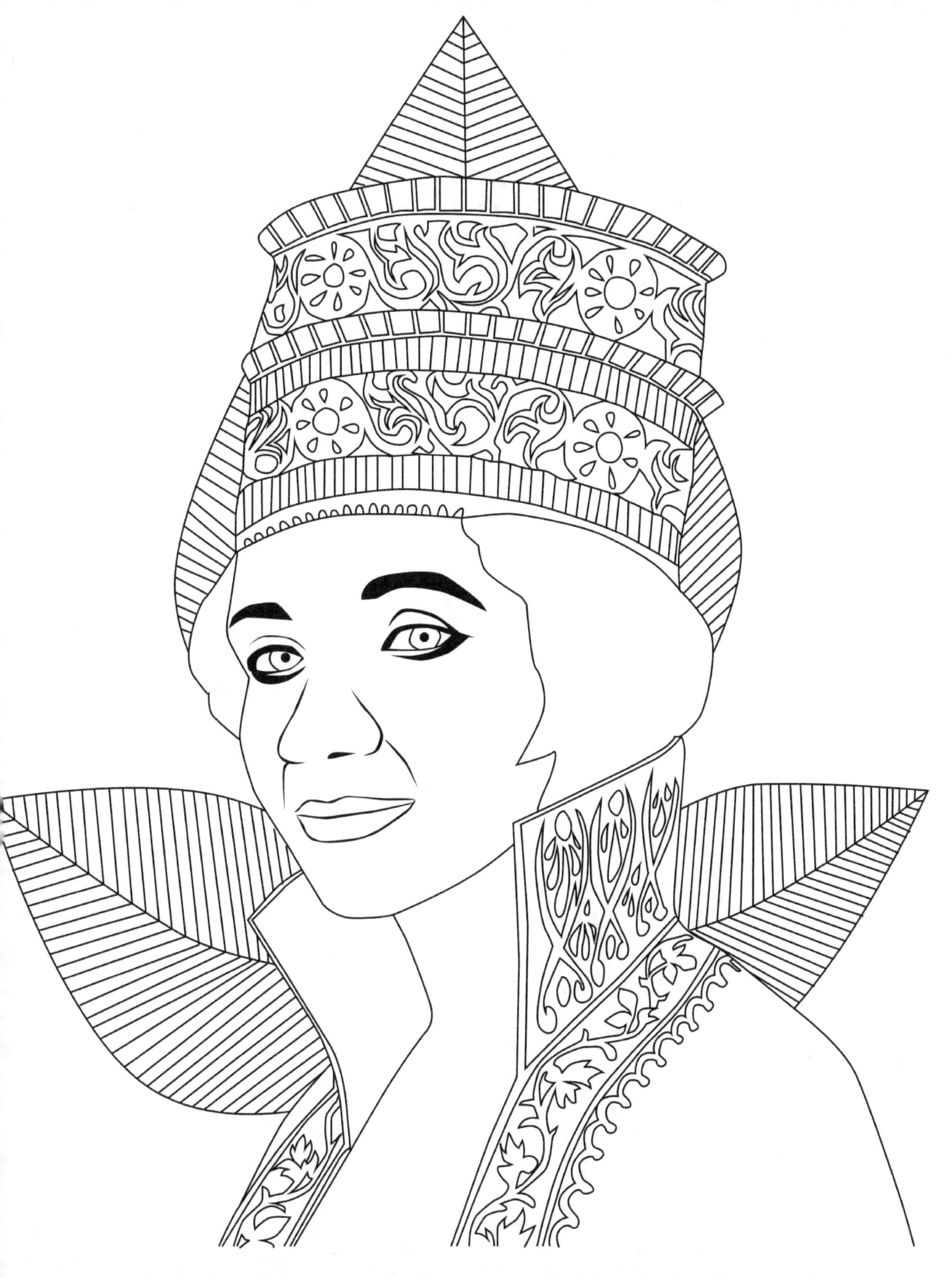

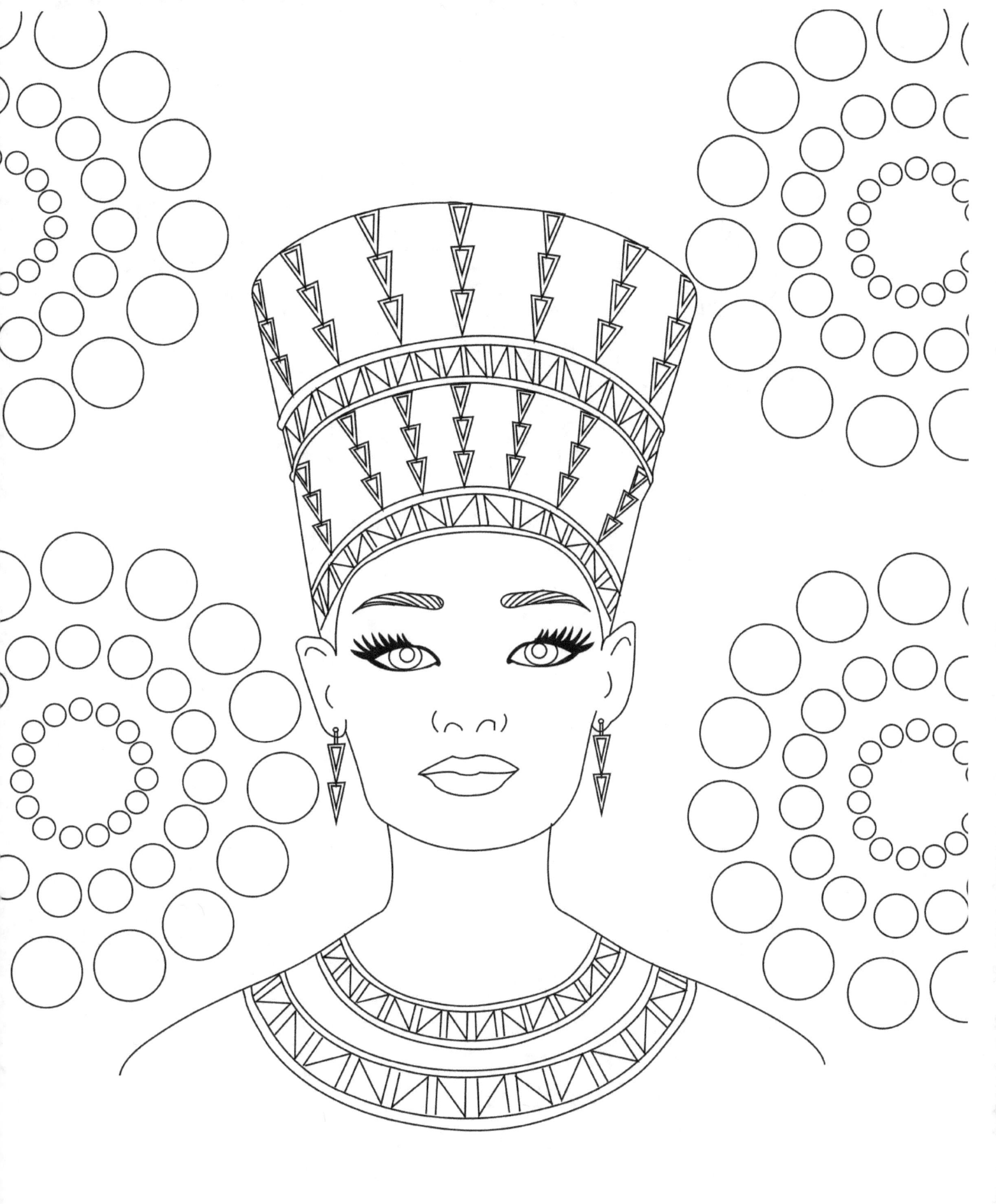

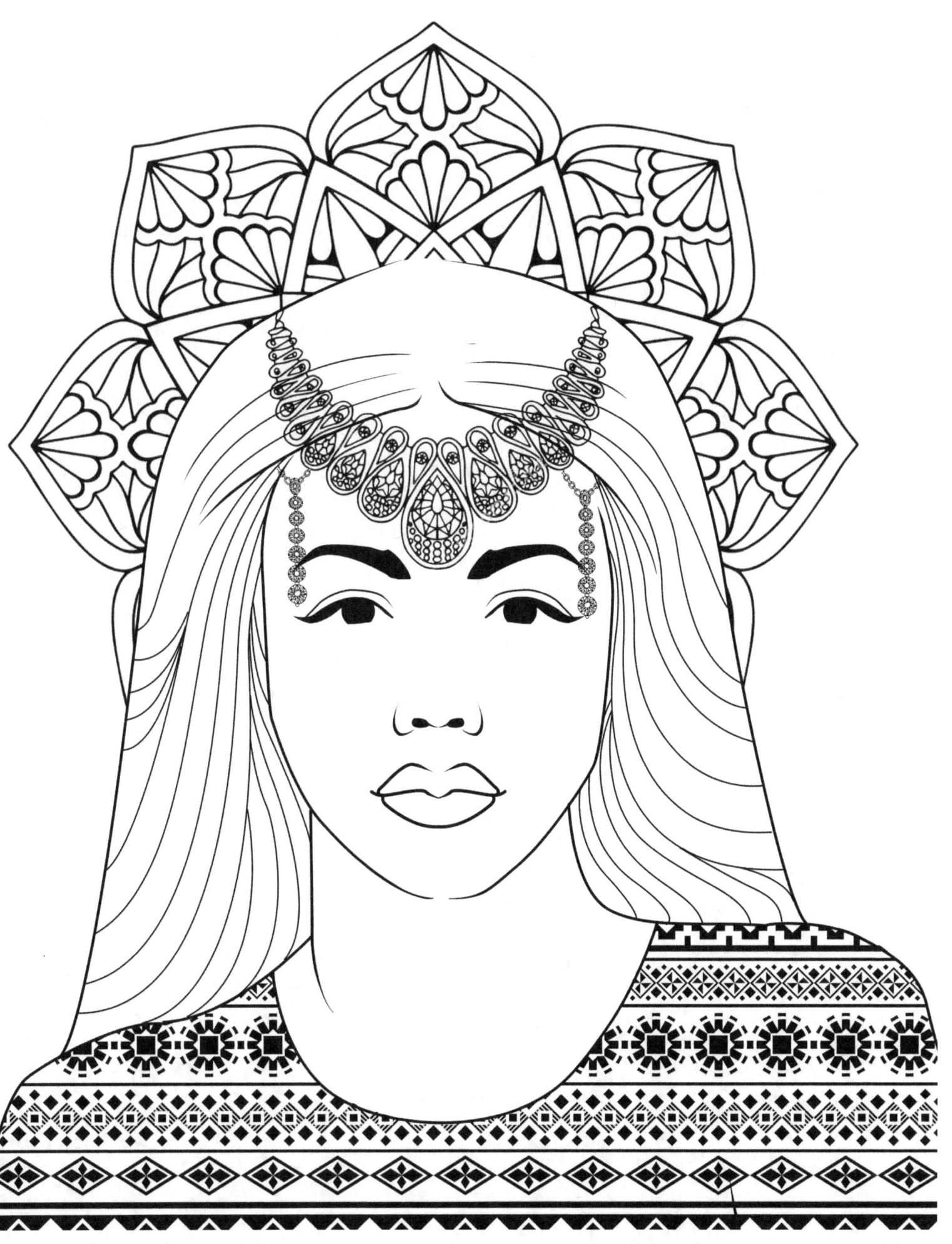

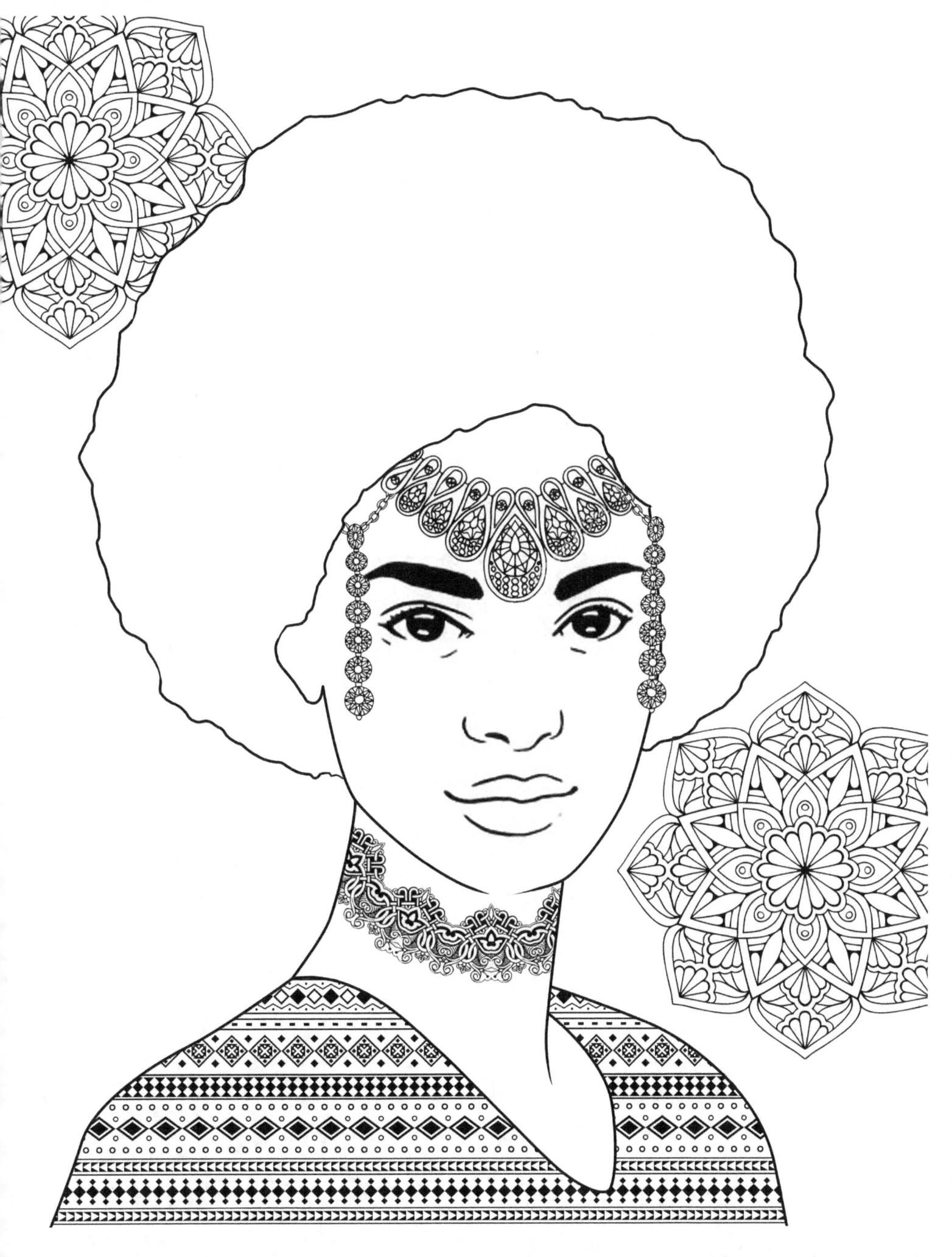

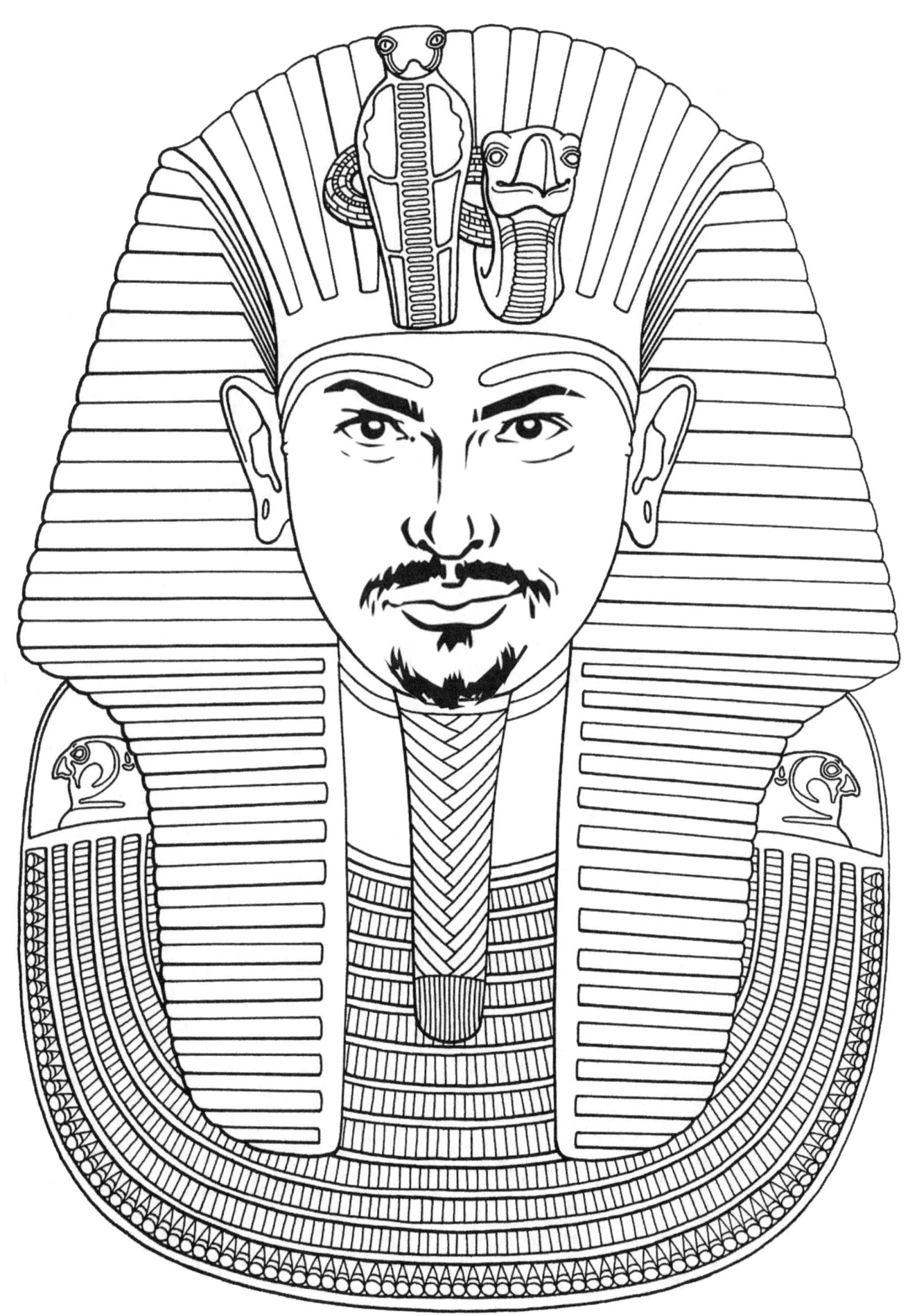

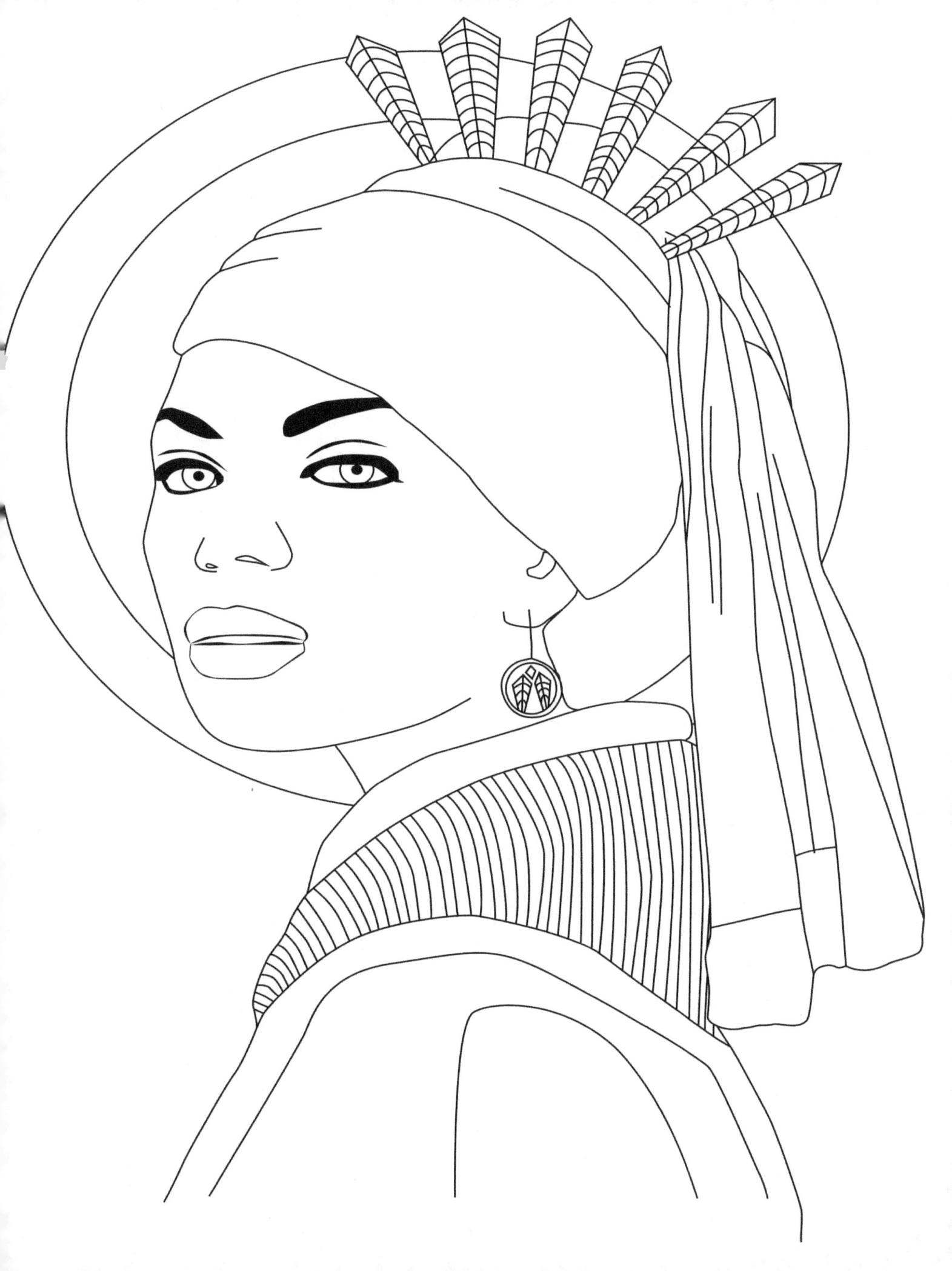

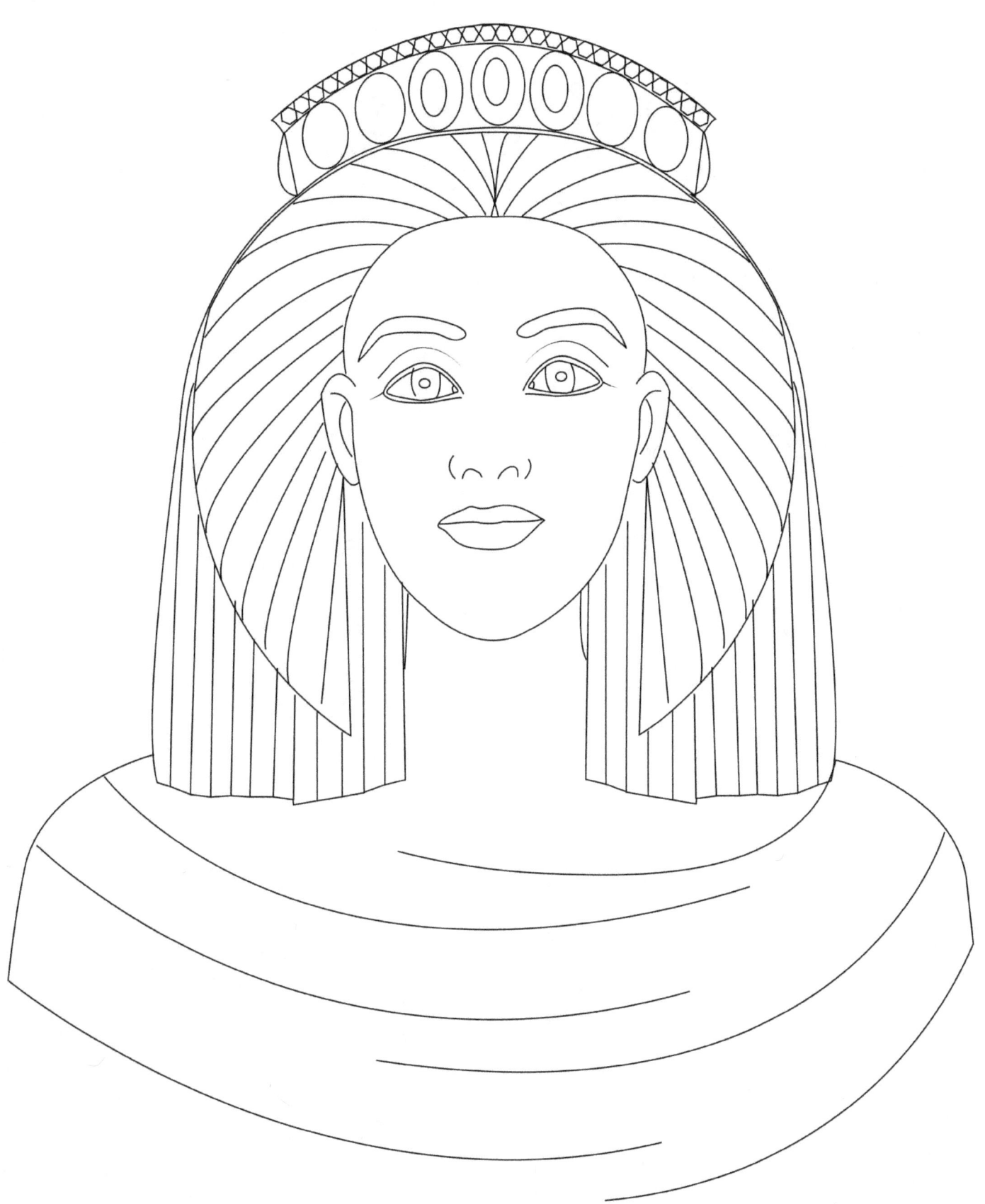

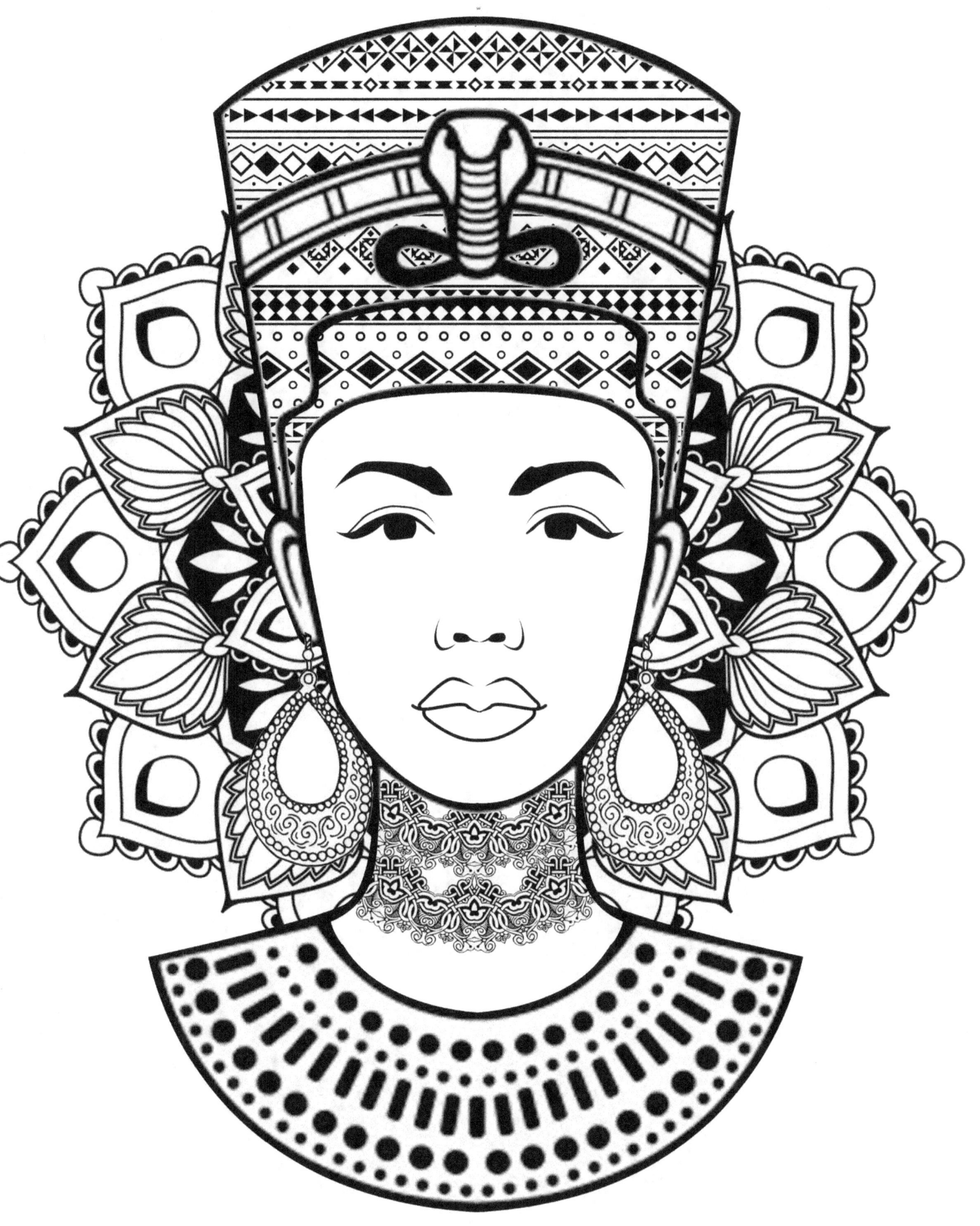

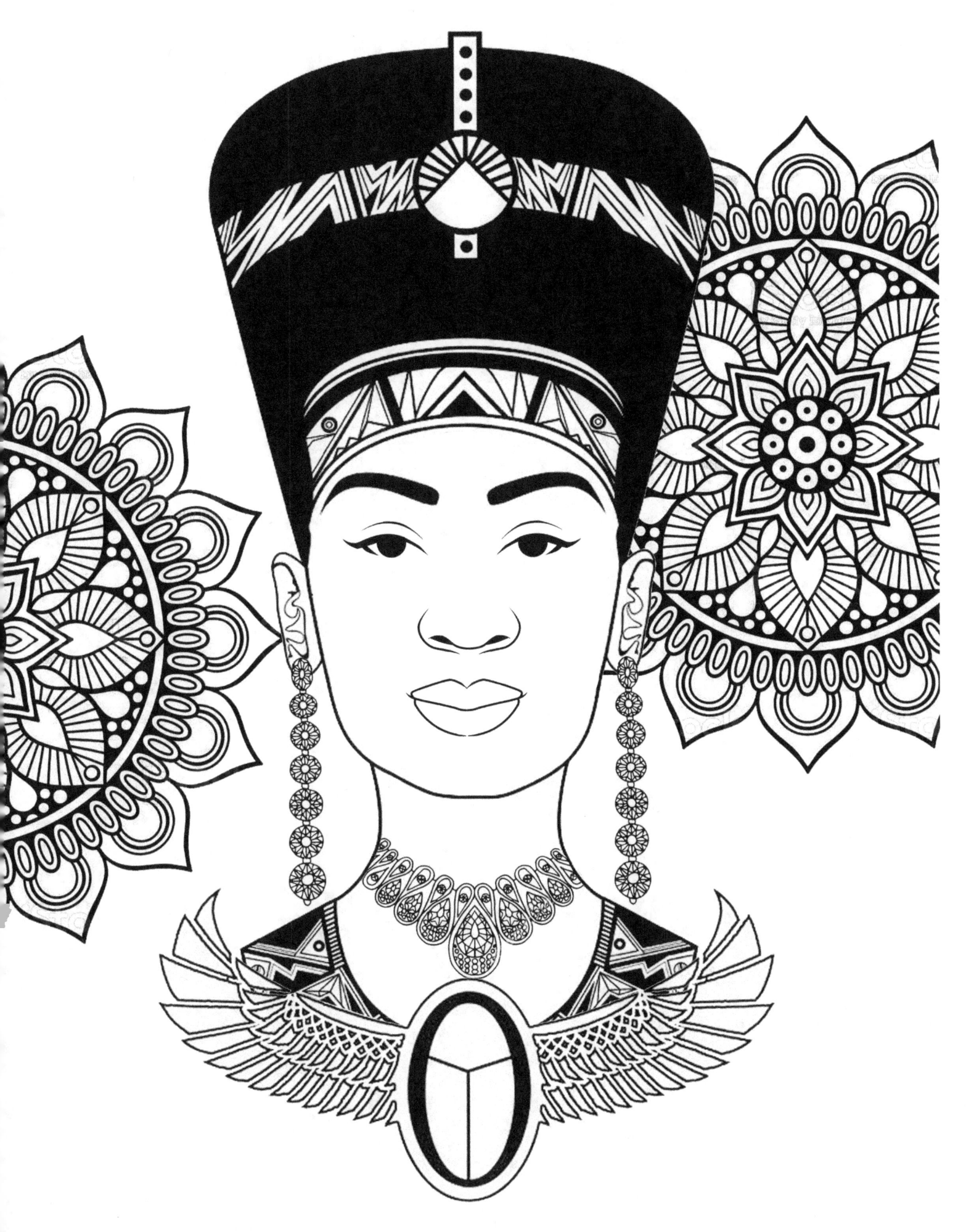

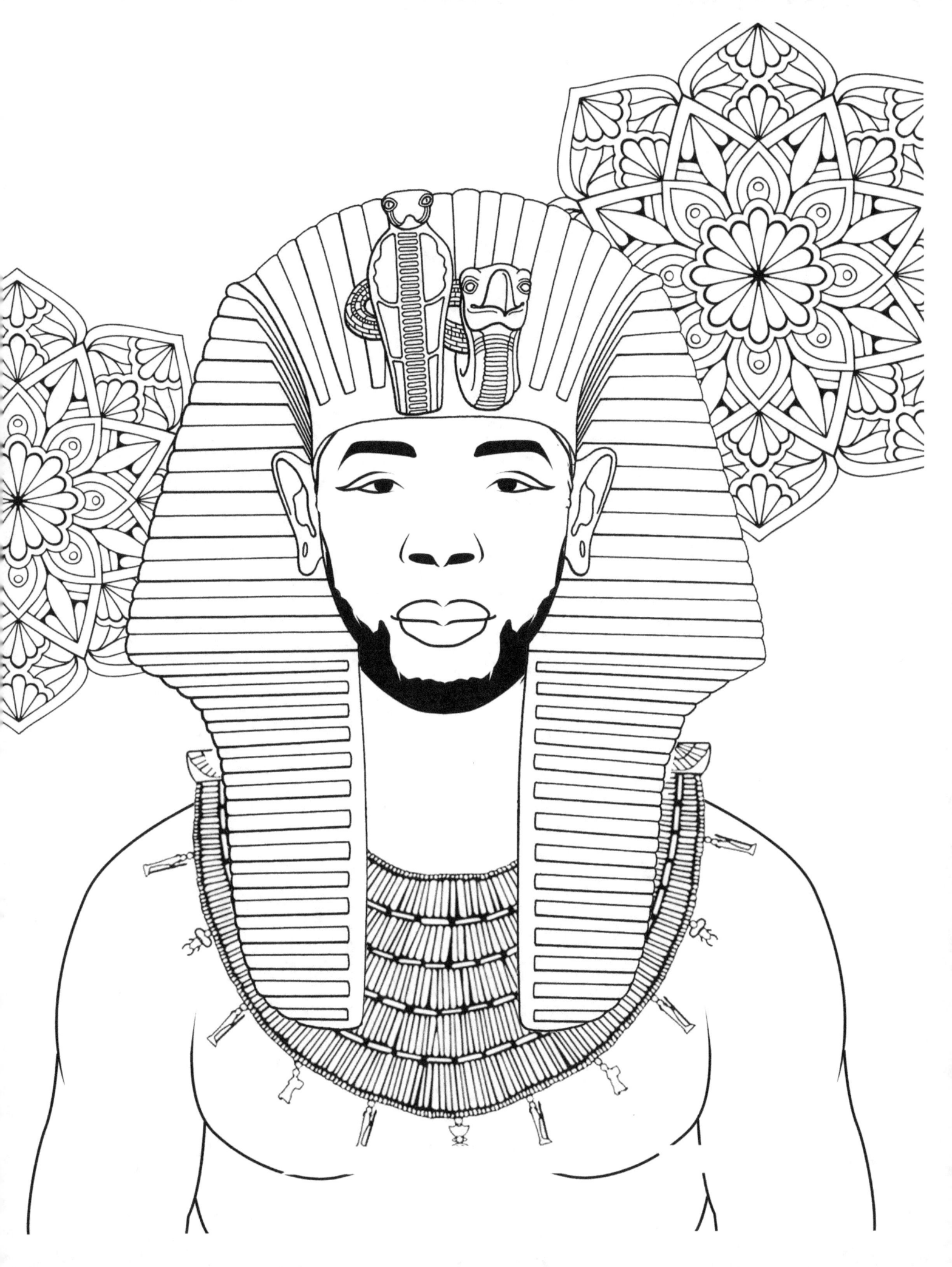

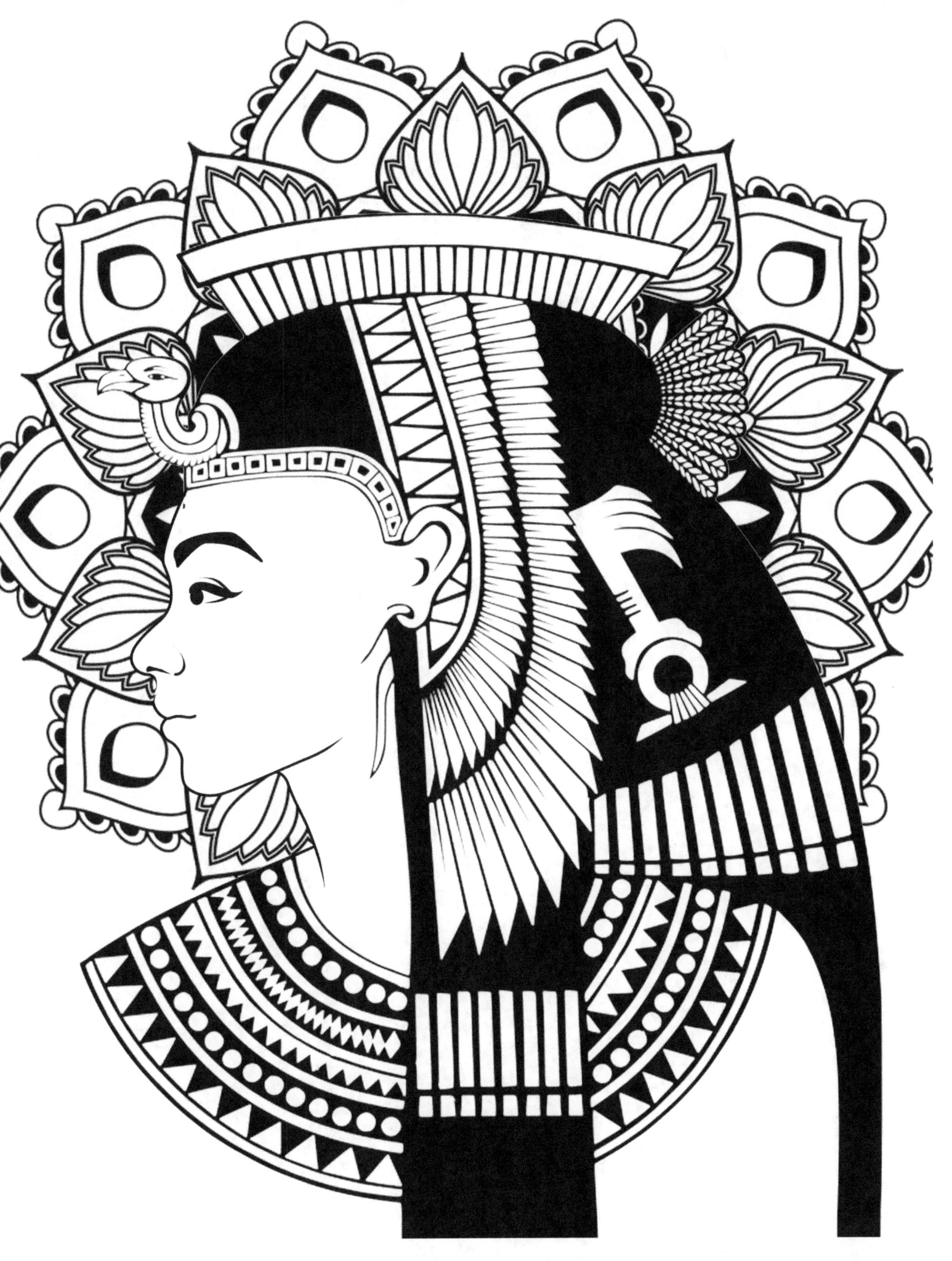

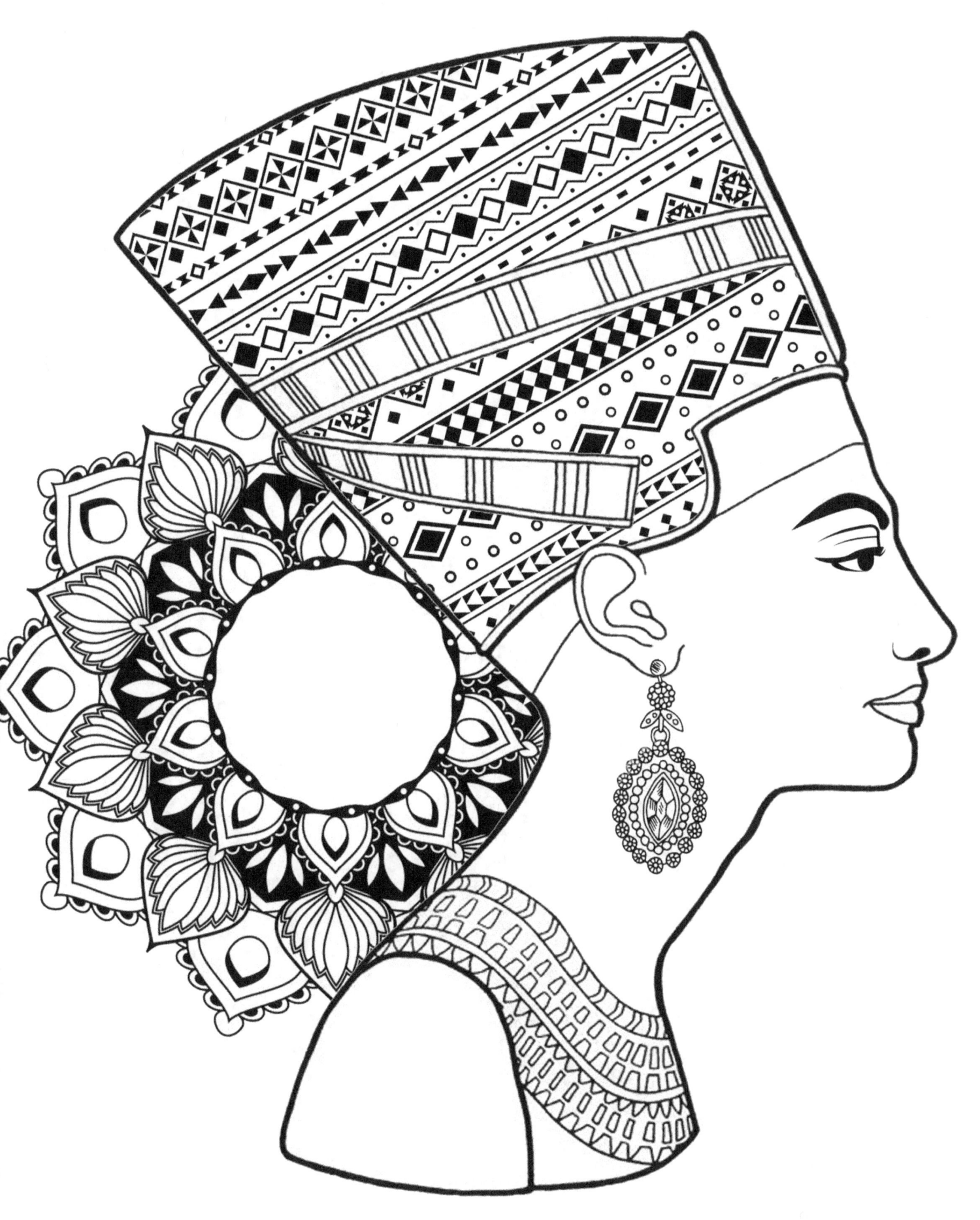

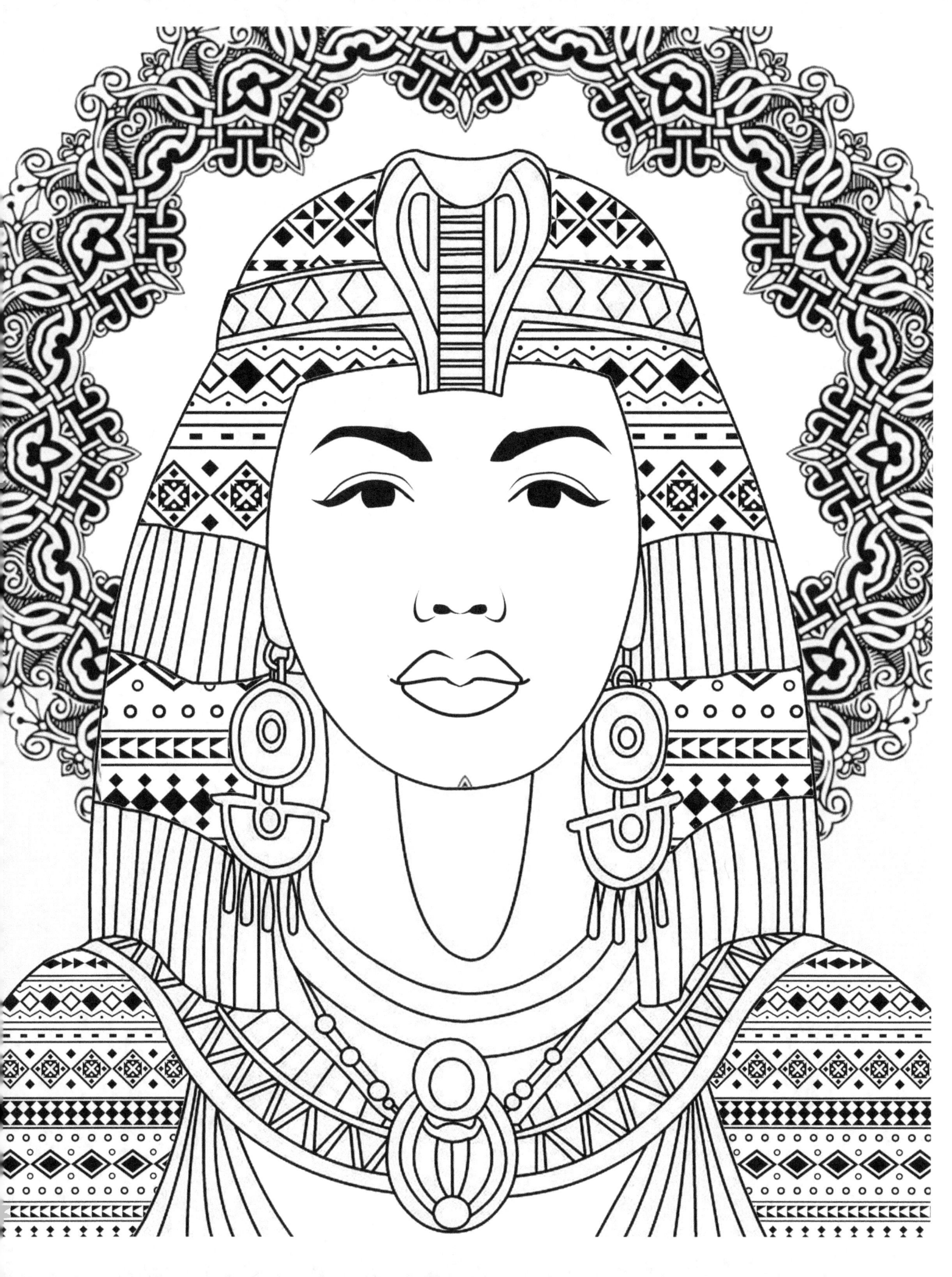

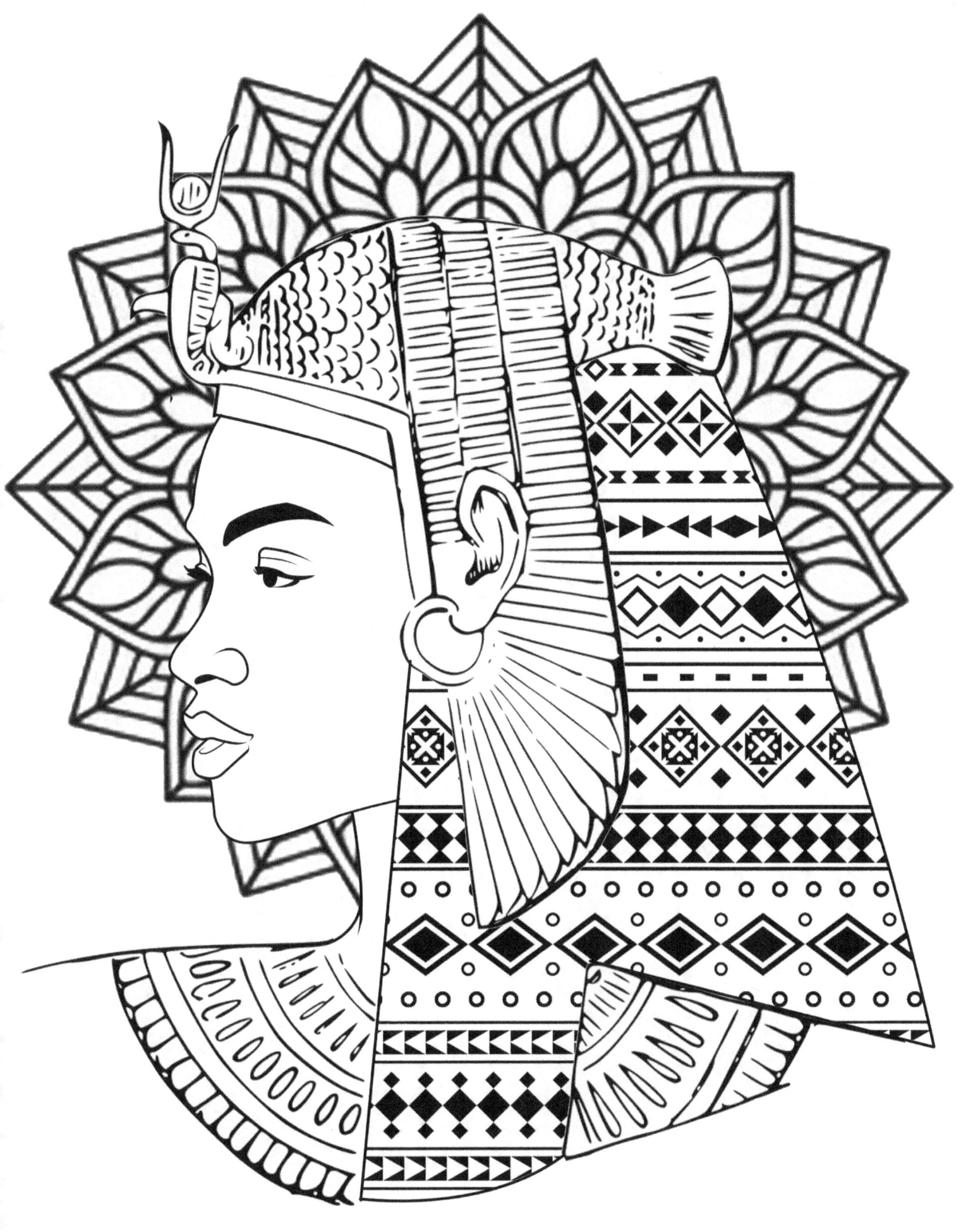

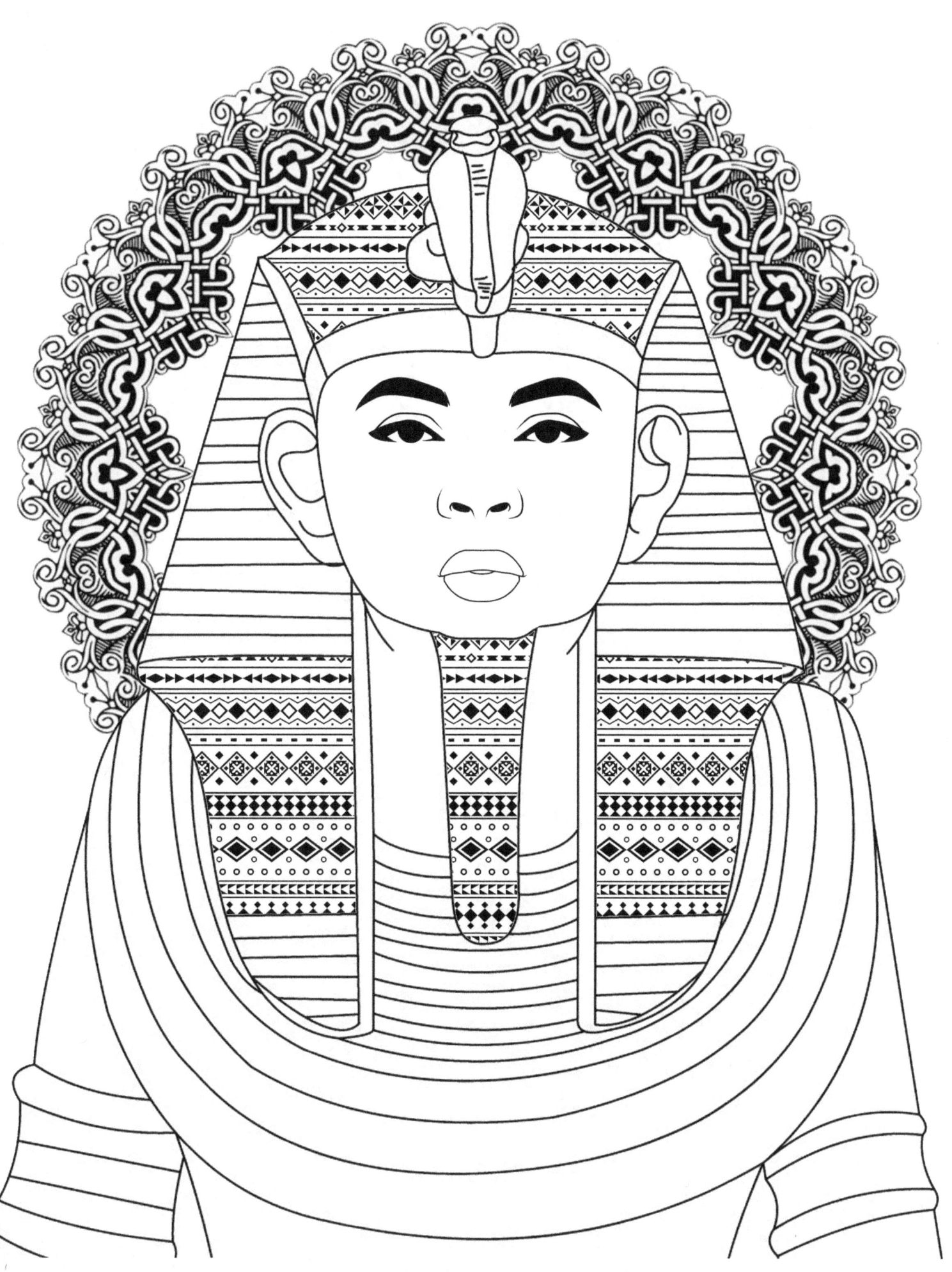

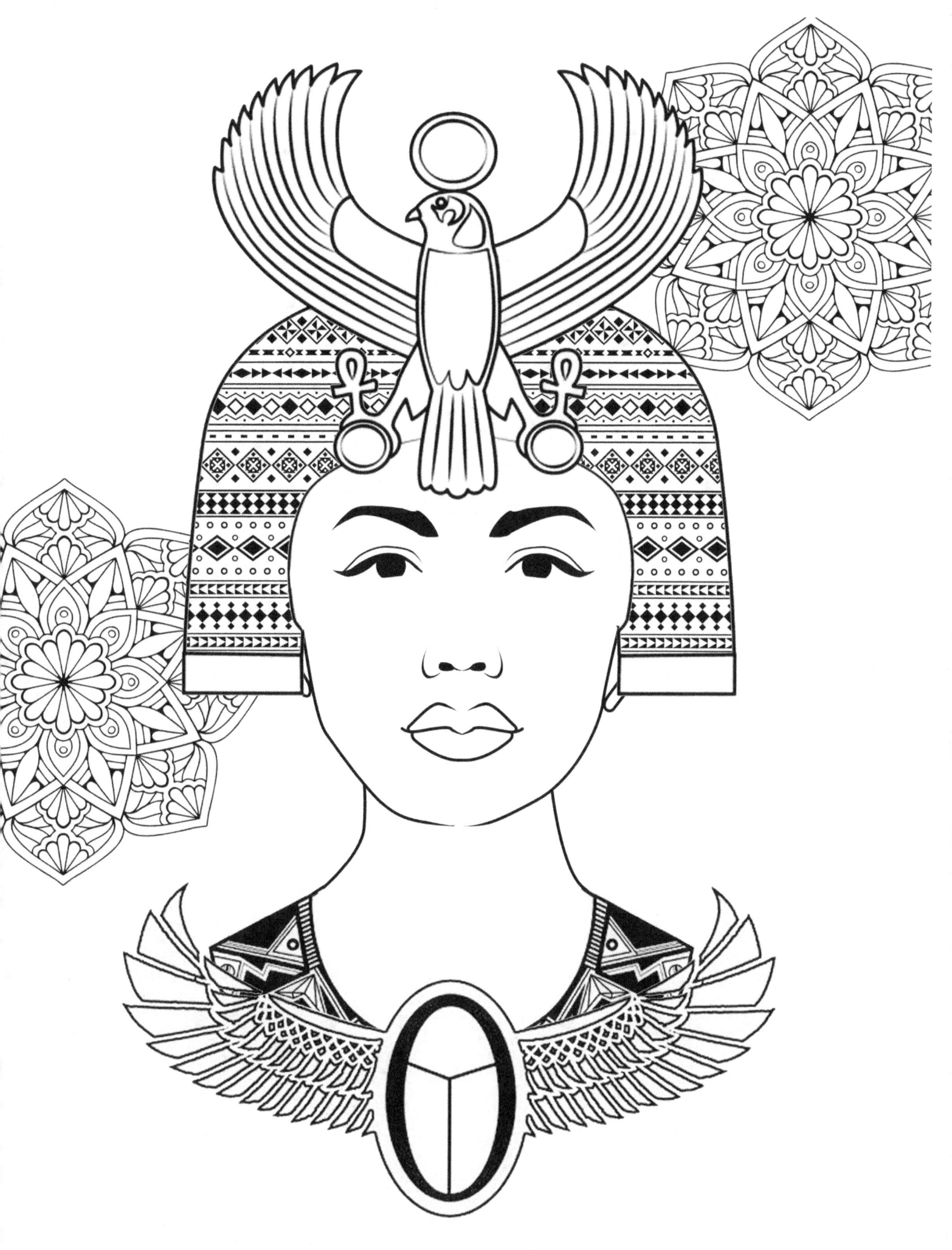

Other Coloring Books from Aryla Publishing

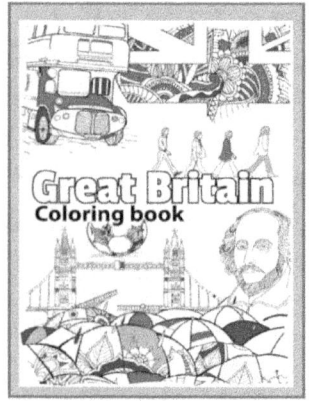
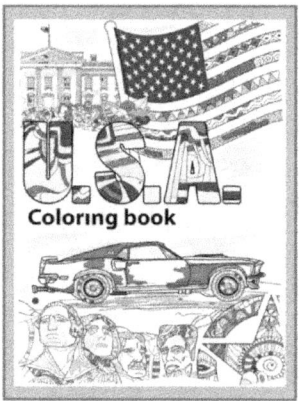
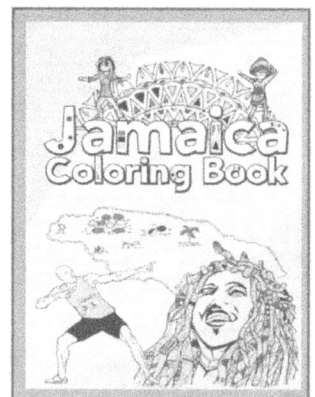
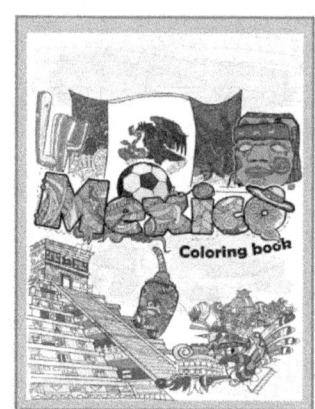

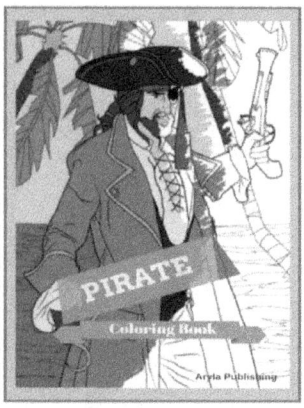
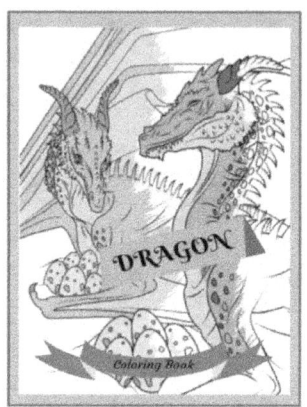
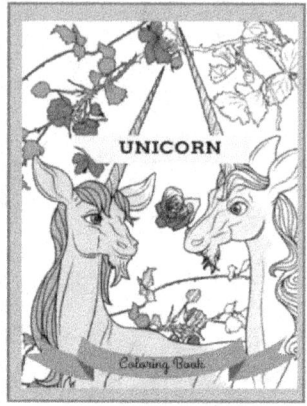
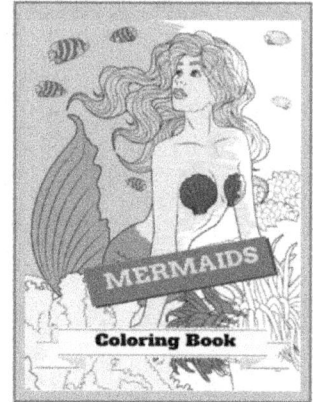

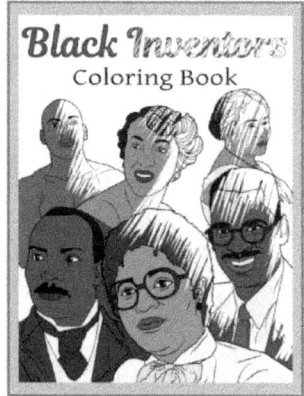
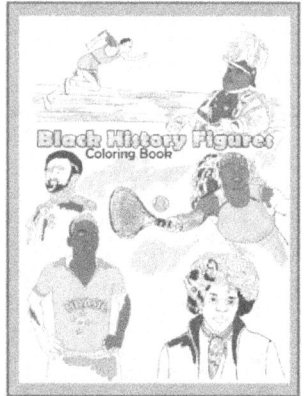
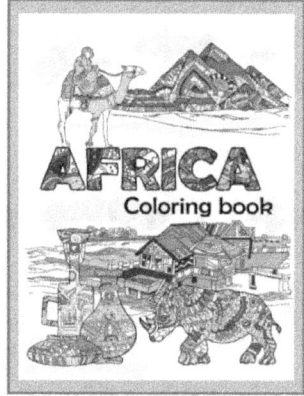
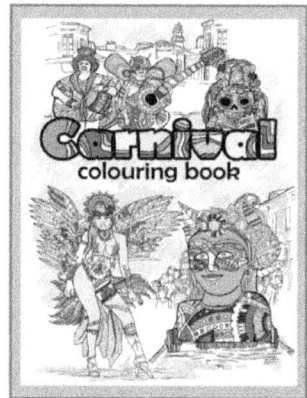

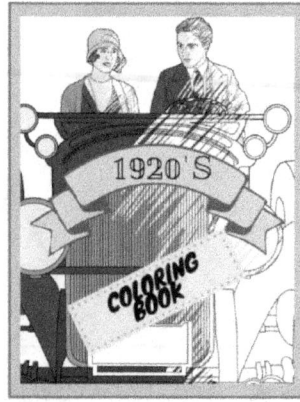
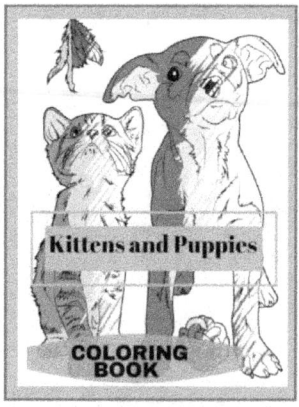
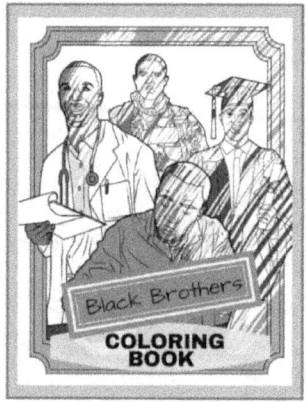
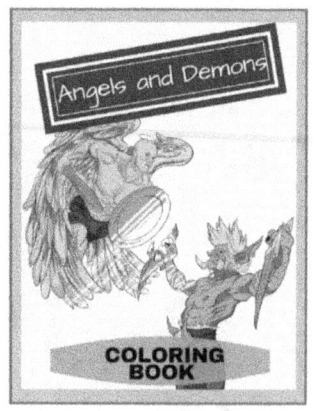

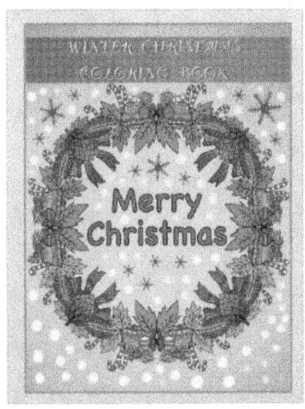

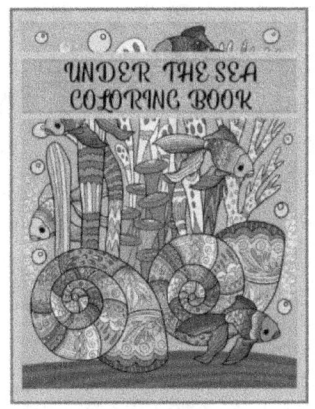

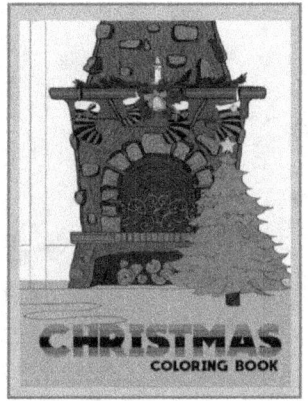

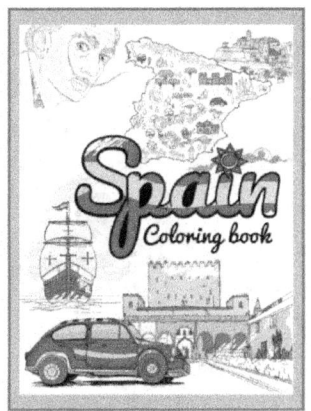

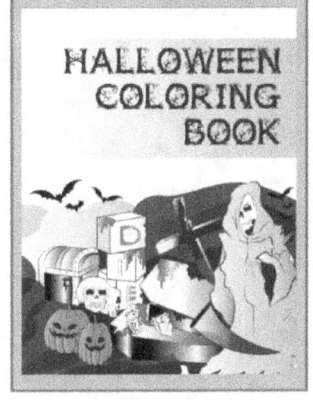

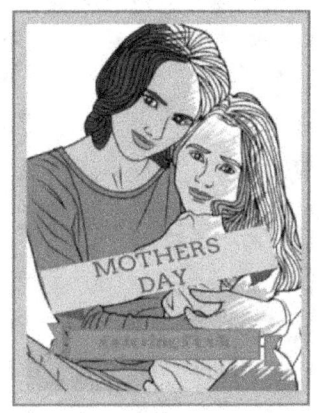

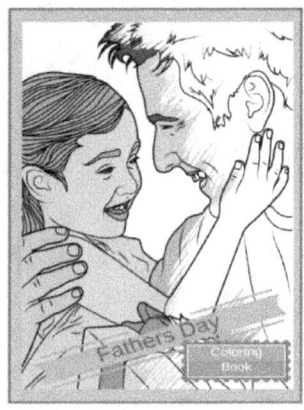

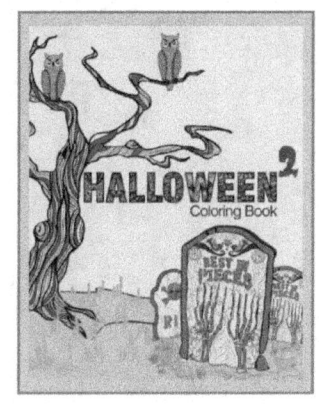

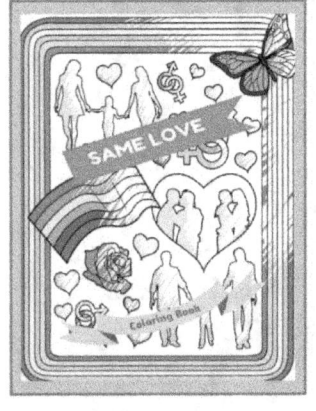

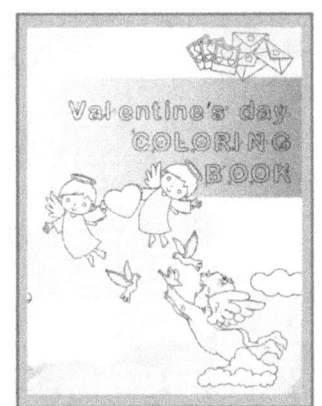

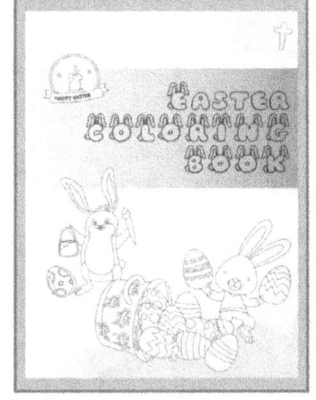

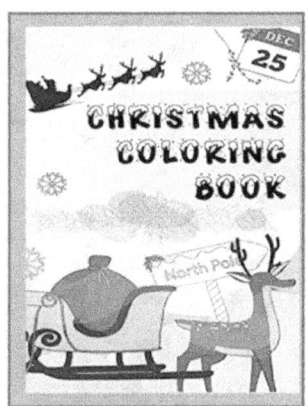

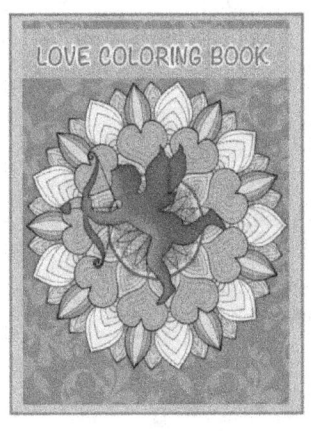

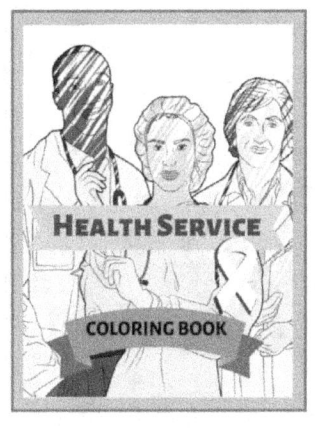

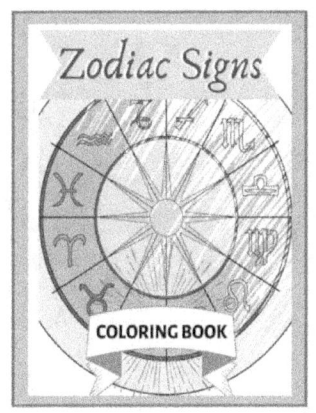

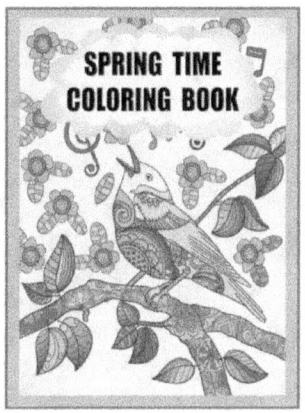

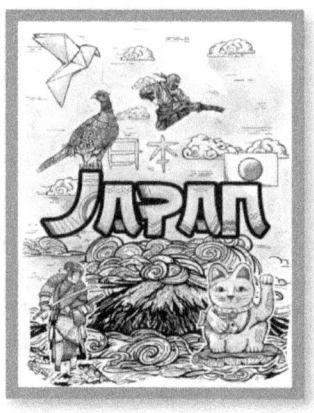

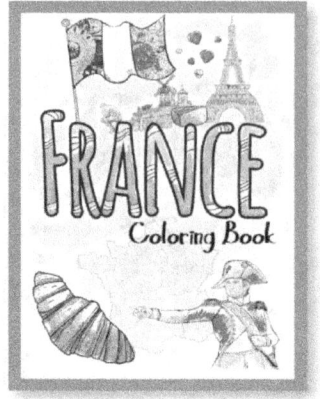

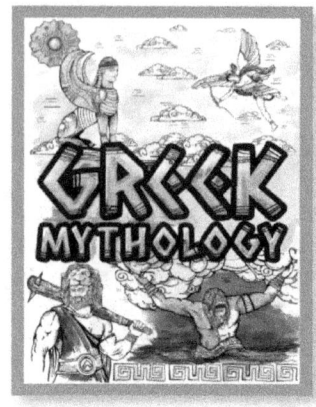

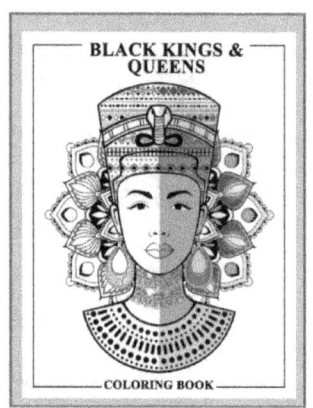

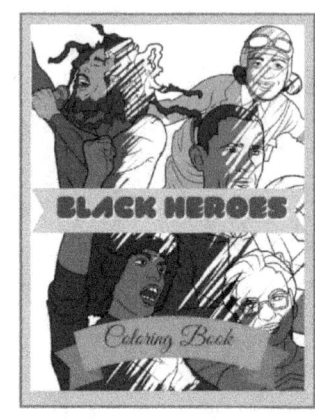

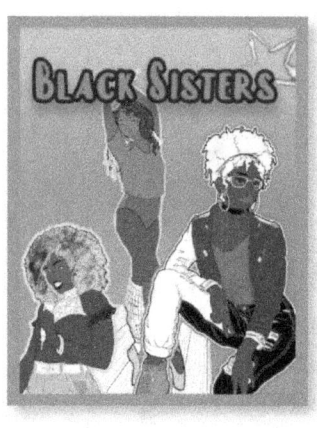

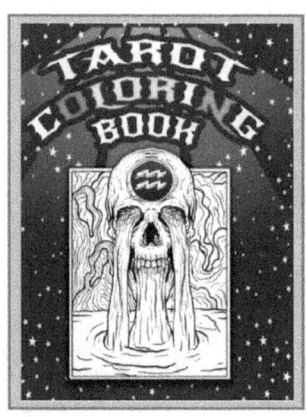

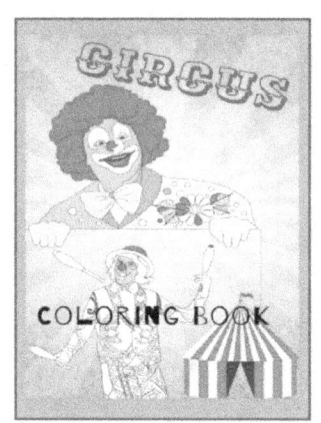

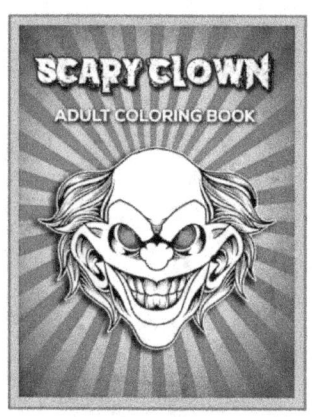

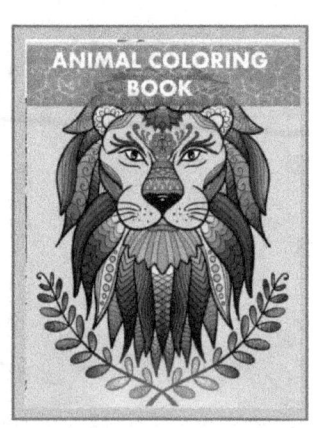

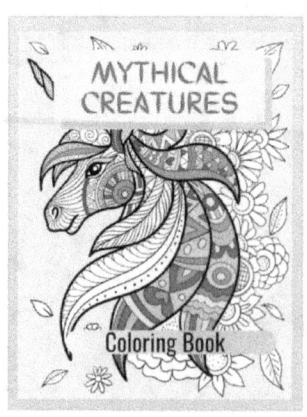

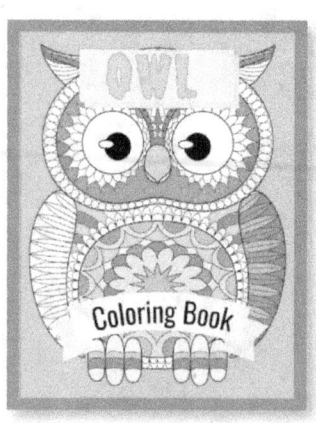

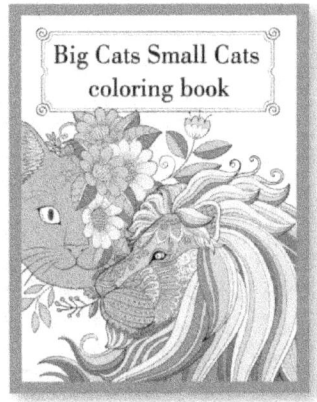

Big Cats Small Cats coloring book

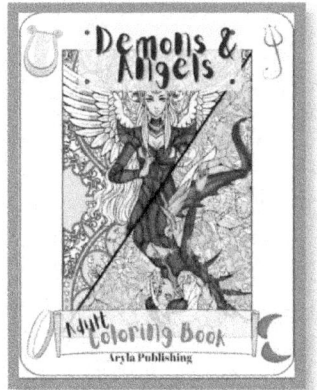

Demons & Angels

Adult Coloring Book

Aryla Publishing

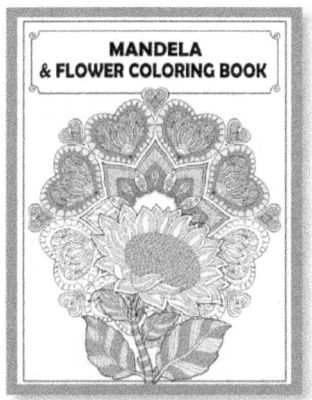

MANDELA & FLOWER COLORING BOOK

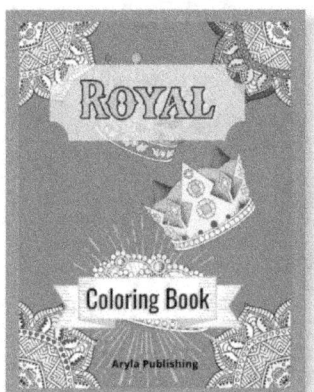

ROYAL

Coloring Book

Aryla Publishing

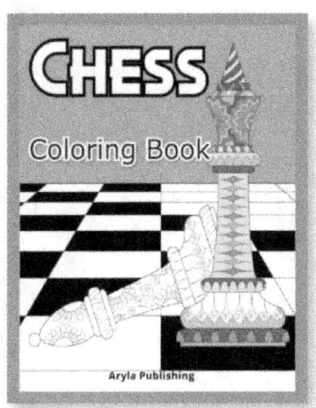

CHESS

Coloring Book

Aryla Publishing

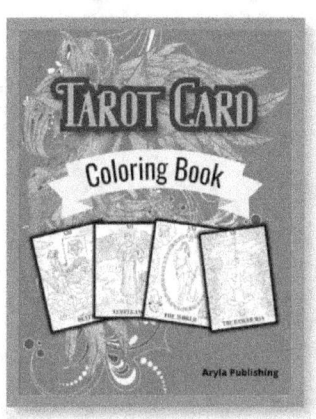

TAROT CARD

Coloring Book

Aryla Publishing

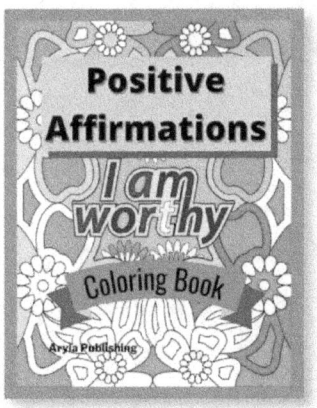

Positive Affirmations

I am worthy

Coloring Book

Aryla Publishing

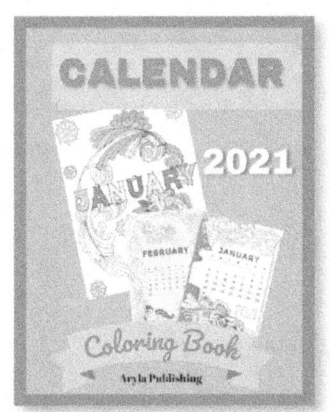

CALENDAR

2021

Coloring Book

Aryla Publishing

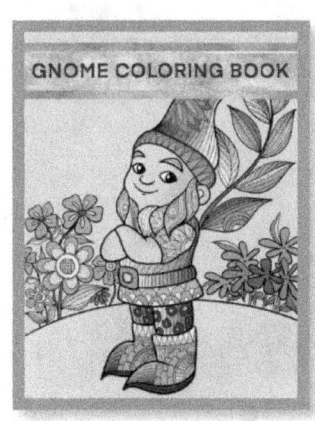

GNOME COLORING BOOK

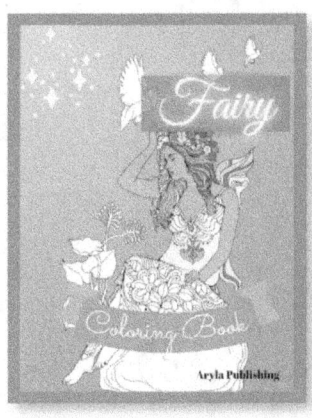

Fairy

Coloring Book

Aryla Publishing

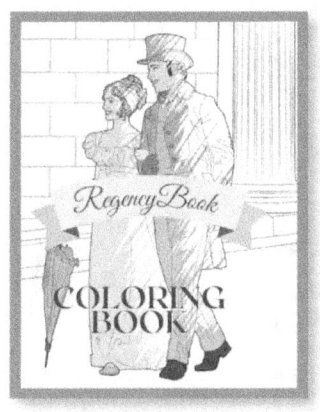

Regency Book

COLORING BOOK

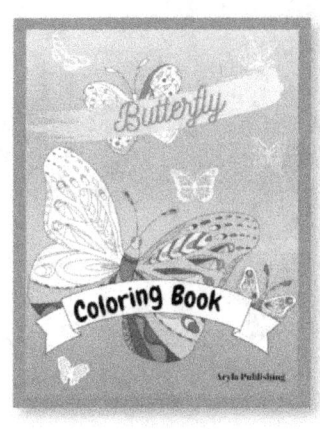

Butterfly

Coloring Book

Aryla Publishing

Color In Fun
Kids Books

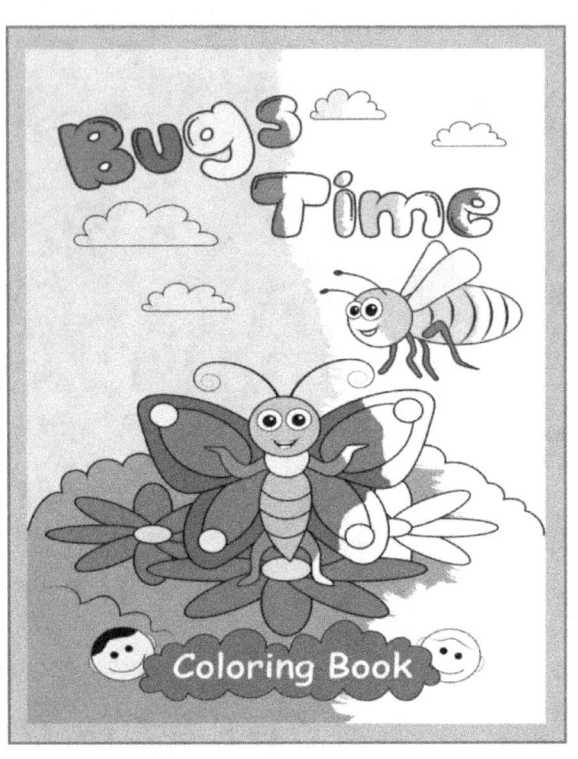

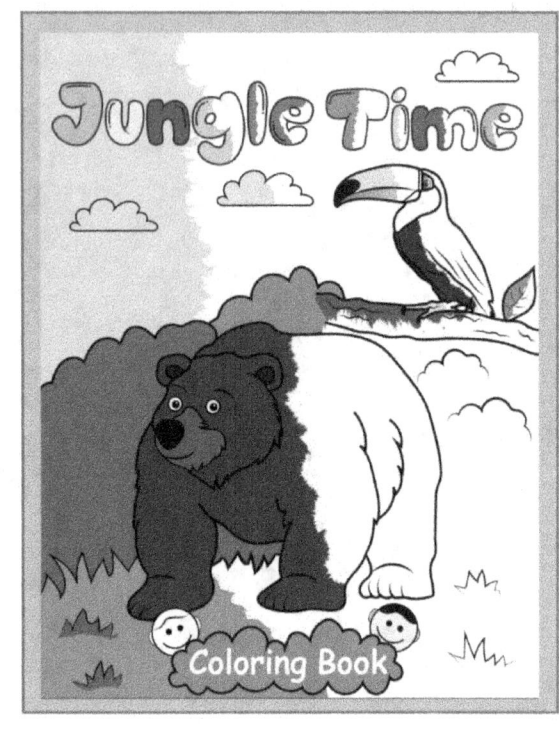

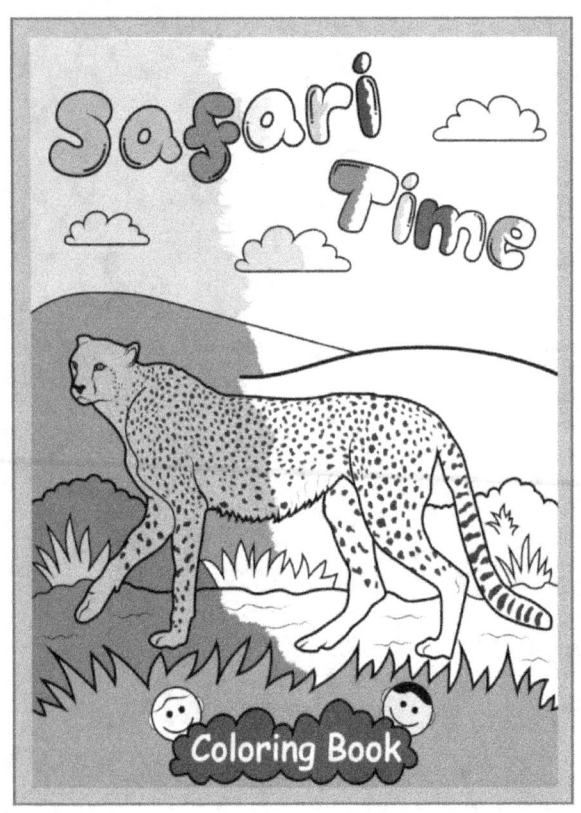

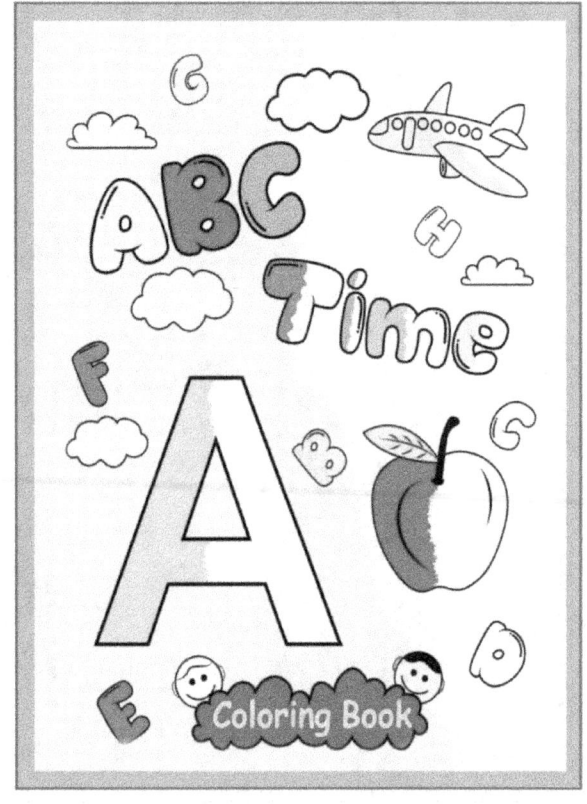

Visit **www.ArylaPublishing.com**
to find out about all new releases.

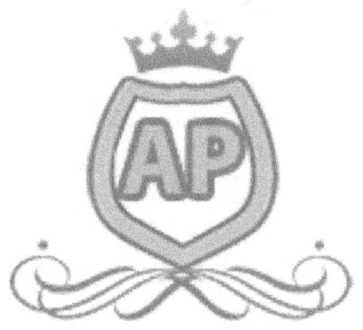

Follow us @arylapublishing on Twitter Instagram & Facebook

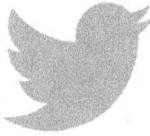  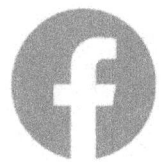

Search for Aryla Publishing on

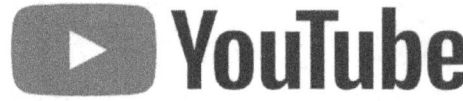 YouTube

Check out our <u>Book Trailers</u>

<u>*Subscribe*</u> **to keep up to date with new releases!**